RICHAR

Notorious

The Maddest and Baddest
Sportsmen on the Planet

HarperSport
An Imprint of HarperCollins*Publishers*

First published in 2006 by
HarperSport
an imprint of HarperCollins
London

© Richard Bath 2006

1

A CIP catalogue record for this book
is available from the British Library

ISBN-13 978-0-00-722485-2
ISBN-10 0-00-722485-0

Illustrations by Hamish Gordon

Set in Sabon by
Rowland Phototypesetting Ltd,
Bury St Edmunds, Suffolk

Printed and bound in Great Britain by
Clays Ltd, St Ives plc

The HarperCollins website address is
www.harpercollins.co.uk

This book is proudly printed on paper which contains wood
from well managed forests, certified in accordance with
the rules of the Forest Stewardshiop Council.
For more information about FSC,
please visit www.fsc-uk.org

Mixed Sources
Product group from well-managed
forests and other controlled sources
www.fsc.org Cert no. SW-COC-1806
© 1996 Forest Stewardship Council
FSC

For Ollie, Ailsa and Lochie

Introduction

I vividly remember the day that this book was born. It was in the autumn of 1993 and I was editing a small rugby magazine when I received a phone call from a French journalist, who proceeded to recount the sorry demise of Armand Vaquerin. It was, quite frankly, such an unbelievable tale of wanton lunacy that I presumed that the writer in question, keen to earn a commission, had been hamming it up in the time-honoured fashion of all freelancers. In fact, quite the opposite was true, and the tale of the French prop's premature death remains a tragically unbeatable tale of sporting excess.

I didn't know at that stage that Vaquerin's folly would launch this tome, but as I discussed the story with my colleague Chris Pilling, we began to chuck around the names of sporting mentalists of every hue. As the process continued over the weeks that followed, and the ranks of Vaquerin's challengers swelled, the extent to which sport is a breeding ground for cranks, eccentrics, obsessives, and psychopaths became increasingly obvious.

Sport spawns individualists of huge self-confidence whose desire to win is so strong that they push their minds and bodies to the outer fringes of sanity. It also provides a Peter Pan environment in which there is a temporary moratorium on the need to grow up and assume the responsibilities and social norms by which the rest of the planet is governed. Crucially, success in sports like football and baseball also provides vast wealth, endless hours to fill and the sort of uncritical adulation that ensures every top sportsperson always has someone on hand to tell him or her how great they are. In such circumstances it is little wonder that some sportsmen and women come to believe that the usual rules simply do not apply. If you don't believe that to be the case, reflect on this: a study by the US National Institute of Mental Health found that between 1988 and 1991 more than one third of sexual assaults committed on American campuses were perpetrated by students on sports scholarships, who account for less than two per cent of students.

Like all projects, this one has mutated. It started off as a quest to find the most unhinged sporting practitioners in history but morphed as it became clear that a list of 100 Vinnie Jones-style hardmen would constitute a one-dimensional bore. Anyway, in the colloquial sense madness is a subjective term which encompasses everything from outrageous heroism through extreme eccentricity to profound psychological trauma. The selection of the following 100 men and women (and despite a conscious effort to spread the net across all sports, circumstances, countries and genders, these pages are dominated by Anglophone men) represents an effort to include as many sporting forms as possible of the mental short-circuiting we know as madness.

I tried to set myself some ground-rules, although readers will undoubtedly argue that I've included exceptions to each of my rules, and in some cases they will probably be right. I decided, for instance, that simply doing a crazy sport – sky-diving, cave-diving, drag-racing, mountain-climbing, ultra-distance running and the like – couldn't be a sign of madness on its own. Otherwise this book would just be a collection of athletes who do remarkable things rather than athletes who are themselves remarkable. It is, I feel, a crucial distinction.

The abiding principle in compiling this list of my 100 biggest loonies is that all of the people in the following pages have either acted in a consistently irrational manner or have demonstrated that they are capable of extraordinary responses to extraordinary situations. That, I suppose, is as close to an objective definition of madness as I am willing to offer. Over and above that, all 100 of the individuals in these pages have stories that have touched me in some way, usually by prompting a macabre and wholly reprehensible freak-show fascination.

I've tried to be as inclusive as possible, neither dismissing individuals because their stories are so well known – Diego Maradona, Paul Gascoigne, George Best, Eric

Introduction

Cantona, Roy Keane, and Alex Higgins all come into that category – nor avoiding fringe figures like Rollen Stewart and Pretty Boy Shaw who exist on the very margins of sport. I was surprised, however, by the degree to which there seems to be a correlation between madness and genius. Or perhaps it's just that the memory of crazy deeds perpetrated by sport's colossuses lingers longer in the memory and in the archives. The other major surprise was the degree to which some unexpected sports churn out the warped and depraved, while others simply don't. For every rugby-playing fruitcake, there are ten baseballing lunatics. As the Yanks would say, go figure.

I have also to thank those friends and colleagues who have helped me research this book or read over sections and provided feedback. Vicky Stirling deserves a medal for listening to me droning on about nutters and for providing her frank opinions on the merits of the lunatics upon whom I eventually alighted. I started off with a list of around sixty sportsmen and women who I thought would pass muster, but less than half of those made the final cut. More than twenty of the seventy nutcases I subsequently found while researching the nooks and crannies of sporting insanity were suggestions from friends and colleagues. For their input I'm truly grateful.

In particular I'd like to thank Jon Hotten, whose fascination with sport's macabre twilight zone and whose willingness to give of his time and surprisingly deep well of knowledge was much appreciated. The following colleagues also gave up time and ideas, and deserve acknowledgement for their input: Craig Lord, Dermot Crowe, Jon Rendall, Iain Fletcher, Mark Woods, Martin Gillingham, Jeremy Hart, James Allen, James Eastham, Stuart Weir, James Hipwell, Richard Verrow, Gary Sutherland, Ciaran O'Raillaigh, Rick Weber, Mark Woods, Neil Forsyth, Rob Eyton-Jones, Gulu Ezekiel, Jonathan Dyson, Peter Roebuck, Alix Ramsay, Harry Miltner, Ivan Goldman, Neil Jameson, Phil Ball, Dan Brennan, Richard Fletcher, Stuart Cosgrove, Dominic Calder-Smith, Gregor Paul, Tom English, Alex Massie, Steve Downes, Eamon Lynch, Matt Zeysing, Michele Verroken, Bill Lothian, Alistair Hignell, Lucinda Rivers, John Huggan and Alan Pearey. My apologies to anyone I've missed out.

I'd also like to thank my wife Bea and beloved kids Ollie, Ailsa and Lochie, who all displayed characteristic forbearance at my continual absences during this work's troublesome gestation. This book is for my three little nutcases.

Finally, I'd like to thank my agent Mark Stanton and my publisher Michael Doggart, without whom this book would have remained an argument between two blokes on barstools.

Richard Bath
Edinburgh
May 2006
(richardbbath@yahoo.co.uk)

PARINYA CHAROENPHOL

Lady-boy killer

The Thai people might have an ambivalent attitude towards sexuality, but there's no doubt that Thai kick boxing, or Muay Thai, is among the world's hardest – and most masculine – of sports. That makes Parinya something of an oddity because from his first bout as a young boy aged 12 one of the most talented kick boxers in the sport's history fought solely to get the money for a sex-change operation. As a youthful Parinya said: 'I've set out to master the most masculine and lethal sport to achieve my goal of total femininity'.

As the fourth of five children of itinerant labourers, Parinya was taught to kick box by his father, who feared that his little boy – who favoured girly scrapbooks and painted nails from an early age, and spent much of his spare time with the village transsexual – would be picked upon. Although Parinya says that 'I don't equate femininity with weakness', Thai kick boxing is a stoically masculine world: women are not allowed to enter a kick boxing ring, let alone fight in one.

Life was hard for Parinya, who became a monk for three years from the age of seven when his mother was

jailed for illegally collecting firewood. He then survived
for twelve months by wandering through villages begging
alms. Throughout his youth, kick boxing was a refuge
and a defence mechanism, but Parinya made his public
debut aged 12 when he entered a fight in a fair because
there was 500 Baht (£7.50) on offer to the winner. By the
time he was 16 he had gained local notoriety, winning 20
of his 22 fights, most of them by knockout. Over the next
four years he became famous for the flamboyant *coup de
grâce* he delivered after each KO, when he would give
his defeated opponent a consolation kiss as the audience
roared with laughter at the sight of the humiliated loser
rubbing away the lipstick. 'The reason I kissed men after
a fight is because it was my way of saying sorry,' said a
deadpan Parinya.

Parinya made his big-time debut in front of 10,000
screaming homophobes in Bangkok's Lumpini Stadium
aged 17. Wearing make-up and pink nail polish, he broke
down when asked to strip for the weigh-in to prove he had
the usual male accoutrements, although he was eventually
allowed to climb aboard the scales wearing just black
jockeys. He then promptly went out and pummelled the
bejesus out of the over-confident Oven So Boonya – who
had made the mistake of mocking Parinya with a camp
embrace – for five bloody rounds. The end of the mis-
match came when Parinya applied his trademark move,
Crushing Medicine, in which he jumped in the air and

brought his elbow down onto the head of the unfortunate opponent. Yet that flashy denouement hid the real secret of Parinya's success: an adherence to the balletic rituals of the ancient sport and a daily nine-hour exercise regime which saw him go for a 10km run at dawn, followed by half an hour of rope skipping, drills of alternate slugs and kicks to a sandbag, all rounded-off by 300 sit-ups during which his coaches would pummel his belly to harden his six-pack.

The low point of Parinya's career came in 1999, by which stage hormone therapy was beginning to have such a noticeable effect that he asked to be allowed to wear a bra when he fought. That's when Parinya went to Tokyo and fought Kyoko Inoue, a Japanese female wrestler almost double his size, in a freak-show hybrid brawl in which the kick boxer triumphed. But then triumph was normal for Parinya throughout his five-year career as a professional fighter, a career which ended abruptly in 2000 when he had amassed enough money for an oper-ation in which he had his genitals removed and voicebox modified.

And then he became a she, changing his name to Nong Toom and hanging up the gloves forever. Now one of Thailand's biggest stars, Parinya/Nong was last seen earn-ing a living as a 'boxing cabaret artist' and making *Beauti-ful Boxer*, a film of his/her life. (Don't laugh, *Iron Ladies*, a movie about the transvestite volleyball team which won the Thai men's championship in 1996 is still Thailand's biggest grossing film of all time).

JOHN HOPOATE

Finger licking bad

Mad, bad, or just dangerous to tackle? Australian rugby league hardman John Hopoate merits inclusion thanks to his predilection for slipping a rigid digit up opponents' arses on the field of play. It happened four times – thrice against Queensland Cowboys and once against St George-Illawarra – leading to his sacking by Wests Tigers after NRL (National Rugby League) commissioner Jim Hall said that 'in my forty-five years in rugby league, never have I come across a more disgusting act.'

Hopoate, who was caught on film inserting his finger all the way up to the knuckle, thought it was all a bit of a laugh, but then maybe he was just trying to fit in because he was playing against North Queensland Cowboys, an outfit who play in an area of the country Aussies call the Deep North, an agricultural region where men are men and sheep are petrified. Even Hopoate's team-mates thought it was a riot: Tigers coach Terry Lamb was particularly amused after watching the video tape of the

St George game. 'Everyone had a big laugh,' said Lamb. 'We thought it was okay because Hoppa's good mates with Craig [Smith, the St George captain and a victim]. We thought it was a gee-up.'

His victims, however, weren't so impressed. 'I couldn't believe it. It felt like he made an attempt to stick his hand up my arse. I shit myself,' said Smith. The Cowboys' captain Peter Jones was also in no doubt that it wasn't funny: 'It wasn't a wedgie. That's when your pants are pulled up your arse. I think I know the difference between a wedgie and someone sticking their finger up my arse.' A third victim, Paul Bowman, said that 'if Hoppa was a man, he wouldn't do this', but Bowman's coach Terry Hall thought it was all a storm in a teacup: 'Things were much worse in my day: I've had blokes grab my family jewels, blokes gouge me, blokes pull my hair. Hoppa hasn't hurt a bloke for Christ's sake.'

One bloke who managed to see the funny side was Ian Roberts, one of Aussie Rugby League's greats, who withdrew from the disciplinary panel citing 'a conflict of interests . . . with three sweaty men and anal penetration it sounded like a gay party to me'. Roberts was, at that time, the League's only openly gay player.

One other player took Hoppa's example to heart. In 2002, the year after Hoppa's strange behaviour first surfaced, 25-year-old Old Trinity Aussie Rules footballer Glen Hatfield was banned *sine die* for emulating his hero in a match against Melbourne High School Old Boys.

Since Hopoate was banned and then fired by Wests, things haven't got better for the rogue. After finally getting back into the game, he was almost sacked by Manly after he was banned for abusing match officials, after which he was forced to issue a grovelling apology for abusing a ballboy during a match against the New Zealand Warriors in March 2005. He was finally sacked by Manly after he was banned for seventeen weeks for a sickening assault which laid out Cronulla Sharks forward Keith Galloway, almost ending Galloway's playing days and killing the 30-year-old Hoppa's career stone dead.

The botty-botherer is now pursuing a career in boxing but still can't keep out of the news. Acting as a waterboy in a match between his teenage son's Manly Cove side and the Western City Tigers in the Sydney Rugby League's under-13 cup in 2005, he was banned from the touchline for abusing officials. According to officials, Hoppa first swore at the referee and touch judges before inviting all three outside for a 'square-go'.

ARMAND VAQUERIN

One madman, one bullet

French rugby props are famously nutty, but few have taken their madness to such violent extremes. Vaquerin may have been capped twenty-six times between 1971 and 1980, and he may have won more French Cup-winners' medals ('Boucliers') with the all-conquering Beziers team than any man alive, but it's for the manner of the loose-head's departure as much as for what he did while he was here that he will be remembered.

Courageous, generous, and famously popular in his home town, Vaquerin had struggled to adapt to life after his rugby career was brought to a premature end in 1980 by a knee injury he first suffered five years earlier (his absence gave Gerard Cholley his chance and the moving brick outhouse quickly established himself as France's premier No.1).

After his retirement, Vaquerin had thrown himself into other sports, notably hunting and deep-sea diving, and had spent six years in Mexico before coming back to his home town, where he opened a bar called Le Cardiff. A larger-than-life bull-necked bruiser with a shiny pate and Pancho Villa moustache, locals said Vaquerin 'liked to live life at 100 kilometres an hour'.

On 10 July 1993, the 42-year-old son of Spanish immigrants organised a party in a local arena to celebrate the twentieth anniversary of his first cap, won against Romania when he was just 20, making him the youngest prop ever to have played international rugby. Despite the fact that a huge crowd had turned up, Vaquerin, who had only had one aperitif, grew restless and went in search of fun.

He crossed to the wrong side of the tracks and wandered into a famously rough Beziers bar and, despite the protestations of friends, proceeded to pick a row with a fellow drinker. The exact sequence of events isn't clear, but it seems that the poor man accidentally spilt Vaquerin's drink, and then offered to buy him another. When the bull-necked prop refused the offer and suggested that they fight instead, the man understandably refused. This is the point at which, to the astonishment of the whole bar, he pulled out a gun from his car and offered his terrified adversary another option: to play Russian roulette with him. Unsurprisingly, the man simply turned and bolted.

Now in the process of having, er, fun, Vaquerin challenged the worried locals to take up his kind offer and join him in a sociable game of blind man's buff with bullets. But when no one would play with him, he took matters into his own hands. Removing five of the six bullets from the chamber of his Smith and Wesson revolver and uttering the immortal words 'if you bastards won't play with me, I'll play by myself', he did just that. The sixth bullet entered his right temple, killing him instantly. Friends said he died as he had lived, in a desperate pursuit of excess.

START FC

Playing for keeps

Sport's ability to make a difference in the most extreme circumstances was demonstrated by the ultimate pyrrhic victory in the midst of the madness that was the eastern front during the Second World War. In arguably the most savage and one-sided David versus Goliath encounters of all time, a bunch of malnourished Ukrainian footballers in rags and shoes took on the mighty Luftwaffe in what became known as The Death Match. It was the classic Catch 22: lose and they betrayed the nation, win and they would face a firing squad or worse. They won.

The 'they' in question was Start FC, the reassembled ashes of the 1939 Dynamo Kiev side which had been one of the best pre-war outfits in Europe, possibly the greatest of Europe's inter-war sides. When the Nazis overran Kiev during Operation Barbarossa, many of the side were dis-

patched to slave labour camps; others, such as Lazar Kogen, were summarily executed.

Many Ukrainians initially doubted that the Nazis could be worse than Stalin, who had a man jailed for ten years for being first to sit down after a standing ovation and had another executed for taking down Stalin's portrait to paint the wall behind it. Yet within a fortnight of taking Kiev, the Nazis had slaughtered 33,000 Jews at Babi Yar and the city's inhabitants understood the horrific nature of an occupation which only 20 per cent of Kiev's inhabitants would survive.

The highest-profile member of that Dynamo Kiev team was Nikolai Trusevich. In late 1941 the charismatic goalkeeper had just been released from an internment camp but was close to death from starvation. As the emaciated figure shuffled around looking for food to keep him alive – every cat, dog and rat in the city had already been eaten – he ran into football-mad Losif Kordik whose reward for collaborating with the Nazis was to be given charge of a large bakery. Not only did Kordik give the former Dynamo captain the job which saved his life, but he also ordered him to scour the city and employ any former team-mates he could find.

When the Nazis allowed football to be played in 1942 in an attempt to normalise life, the bakery owner asked Trusevich to form a team from his fellow workers – almost all of whom were Dynamo men – but many worried they would be seen as collaborators. Trusevich argued the opposite case passionately: 'We may not have weapons but we can fight on the football pitch. We will be playing in the colour of our flag. The fascists should know that our colour cannot be defeated.' And so Start FC was born.

Despite their shambolic physical state, Start beat a team of local collaborators 7–2, then dispatched sides representing occupying forces from Hungary and Romania, the latter 11–0. When Start beat a German unit 6–0 and started to become a focus for Ukrainian pride, alarm-bells sounded and the Germans fielded the best team in the Reich, the Luftwaffe's Flakelf. Start's starving Slavs beat the well-fed Aryan Supermensch 5–1.

Apoplectic, the Germans ordered a replay, which took place before a capacity crowd of Ukrainians and Germans, with 200 Wehrmacht dog handlers in attendance. Nobody harboured any illusions about what another Start win would mean. Just before the match an SS officer walked in and announced that he would be the referee, instructing the Start players to give the Nazi salute before the game. Flakelf saluted to loud roars from the German spectators, but when Start instead clapped their fists to their chests and shouted 'Fitzcult Hura' – ('physical culture' the traditional greeting before any Soviet sporting event) they had signed their death warrants.

When the Ukrainians led 3–1 at half-time, they were

visited by another SS officer. 'You have played very well,' he said. 'And we are very impressed. But you cannot expect to win. I want you to take a moment to think of the consequences.' They did, winning 5–3, with defender Klimenko running almost the whole length of the pitch, through several tackles, to the goal line, but instead of putting the ball into the goal he stopped it on the line; toying with the Master Race and humiliating them in the process. Then he ran into the goal, turned, and kicked the ball back up the field. That's when the referee blew for full-time, more than fifteen minutes early.

Very few Start players escaped, and most were tortured before being dispatched to the great clubhouse in the sky. On the day when Trusevich was finally killed, two Start teammates in his labour camp had already died of wounds inflicted in the torture chamber when he was instructed to line up. A guard, approaching him from behind, tried to use his rifle butt on the back of Trusevich's head but, defiant and agile to the end, he dodged the blow and leapt at the guard screaming: 'Red sport will never die'. Three guns barked: he was dead before he hit the ground.

DAVID ICKE

The Son of Godhead

Forced to retire from football at 21 ('three sevens, an important number in my view' he said mysteriously) because of premature rheumatoid arthritis, Hereford goalkeeper David Icke went on to become a household name as a soccer TV presenter for twelve years. Then, in 1990, he went mad. Absolutely bonkers, in fact. Declaring that he was 'the son of Godhead', he went on to outline quasi-religious beliefs that were more Ron L Hubbard than Glenn Hoddle.

His epiphany was nothing if not amusing. He went onto *Wogan*, dressed from head to foot in turquoise, and told the genial Irishman that: 'in the 1980s when I was a BBC presenter there was this presence close to me. I thought someone else was there. I went to a psychic and she said I would be world famous and was the Son of God – and there I was, presenting the snooker.' Not surprisingly Wogan was a little sceptical and pointed out that the audience were laughing.

'The best way of removing negativity,' Icke said, 'is to laugh and be joyous, Terry. So I am glad that there has been so much laughter in the audience tonight.'

'They're not laughing with you! They're laughing at you!' replied an incredulous Wogan.

Among Icke's more choice utterances was that he had received 'channelled messages' from both a Chinese mandarin, Wang Yee Lee, and from Socrates. He also reckons that the world had been taken over by 12ft blood-drinking, child-abusing alien lizards (the Queen is one, so was her Mum, and so are George Bush, Tony Blair, Hillary Clinton, Kris Kristofferson, and Boxcar Willie). So convinced is he of this that in the wake of the World Trade Center bombings he published a book called *Alice in Wonderland and the World Trade Center Disaster: Why the official story of 9/11 is a monumental lie* in which he outlined an elaborate conspiracy theory about the events of that day, arguing that it was carefully staged by high-ranking members of the Illuminati (reptilian bloodline), including George Bush, Dick Cheney, and Tony Blair. 'Reptiles run the world. I have had dozens of people telling me they've seen important people turning into reptilian humanoid figures. They have nodules on their head and drink human blood, mainly of blonde-haired, blue-eyed people.' When asked about his claim that the Queen is a lizard who drinks human blood and enjoys child sacrifice, he replied: 'If it's not true take me to court. Let's have it out.'

Other nutty pronouncements include the revelation that the planet earth vibrates at the same velocity as turquoise; that Arran, a small and perfectly respectable island off the west coast of Scotland, would fall off the end of the world and into the sea in 1997; and that the Sahara would blossom once more. Not surprisingly, Arran is still as dry as a temperance meeting and the Sahara's still fairly sandy.

Icke's work has involved a great deal of travel in which he has been 'leaving stones and pieces of wood in different places to help unlock the combination set up by Arthur, Avola, and Merlin and so release the Green Dragon energies to the heart chakras of the planet'. We may not know what he's talking about, but the Muans did – they were our predecessor race, who had thin bodies with 'little hair' and long, white soft gowns, and who 'did away with themselves by getting overawed by the spirits of rocks.'

Icke has grown increasingly potty since 1991, setting up a cult on the Isle of Wight and issuing eye-wateringly amusing edicts. As with all sensible latter-day yogis, most of his followers seem to be young, blonde, and female. So maybe there is a method in his rather extreme form of madness. The turquoise-clad one was last seen presenting *Headfuck*, a late night session of weird film clips and music videos on the Sci-Fi channel while simultaneously pretending not to exist any more. 'David Icke does not exist,' said David Icke. 'My name is just a name for what my infinite consciousness is experiencing.' Quite.

DARRYL HENLEY

Living the American Dream

The LA Rams defensive back was never a man to let the grass grow under his feet – well, not without wanting to sell it on. When he began to get a little fed-up with a career in American football that seemed to be more about the taking part than the winning – 'in six seasons we won just thirty-four games; losing became okay and accepted' – he decided that it was time to set up a second career for the time when his $600,000 a year salary dried up.

Being the product of an exclusive private Catholic school and UCLA university, Henley knew how to live the American dream, and also needed to prove he was a leader of men. What better way to combine the two, and to liven up life a little, than by setting up an America-wide drug-smuggling ring with himself at its head.

Things started to unravel in 1993 when Henley's accomplice, a pretty 19-year-old former cheerleader called Tracey Ann Donaho, was arrested by the FBI carrying 12 kilos of cocaine in her luggage. The dealers for whom the coke was destined soon came after Henley, armed with malice aforethought and AK-47s. Rams administrator Jack Faulkner later testified that he saw two 'short, chunky black males' with guns and several

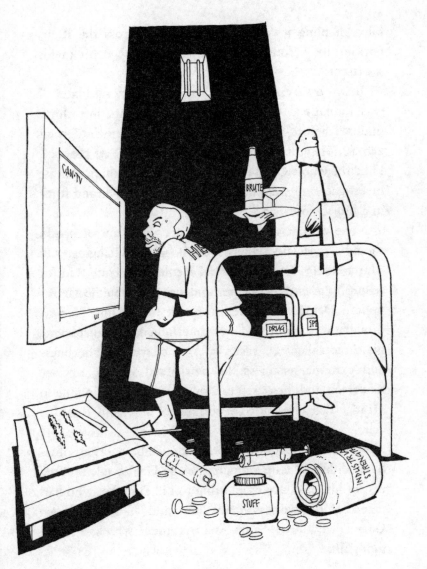

21

kilos of bling jewellery chase Henley across the Rams parking lot before their intended mark sped off in his sportscar.

'It was a very, very difficult time,' Henley said later. 'I was kidnapped one time in training camp, just thirty minutes before bed check. They forced me into their vehicle. They finally let me go at 12.30 a.m. At practice, I had the whole OJ thing. I had secret police there. Private investigators. I was picked up and taken back and forth in a bulletproof Ford.'

None of that was enough to keep him out of prison though, especially when Donaho started singing. On March 28 1995 in Santa Ana, Henley was convicted for selling 50 pounds of cocaine and was placed in the Metropolitan Detention Center to await sentencing. Henley, though, was nothing if not determined, and displaying his three salient characteristics of charm, stubbornness and extreme nastiness, he befriended warder Rodney Anderson and then used the gullible guard's cellphone to arrange deliveries of $1m shipments of heroin from his cell.

Perverting prison warders and peddling drugs obviously didn't take up enough time, so Henley filled up the rest of his existence by plotting to kill Donaho, who had turned State's witness against him, and US District Judge Gary L Taylor, the Santa Ana trial judge who had found him guilty.

Darryl Henley

Unfortunately for Henley, not everybody found him as charming as his pet warder. When his tiresome boasts about being 'Da Man' wore thin on fellow inmates, they grassed on him. Predictably for such an inept criminal, the men on the outside with whom he was dealing turned out to be undercover FBI agents who later testified that they set up $1m of sham drug deals with Henley and the guard, adding that Henley offered then $100,000 per hit to 'whack' Judge Taylor and Donaho. Another outside accomplice, brother Eric, was also arrested and sentenced to five years in jail.

In March 1997, Henley received forty-one years for trafficking and plotting to kill Donaho and Taylor. 'It is obvious that he [Henley] is even more dangerous in custody than out of custody,' said judge Idelman at his trial. 'If there was ever a guy who needed to be locked down twenty-four hours a day, it's Henley. If the court was sentencing Mr Henley, the sentence would be different, I assure you. The defendant is obviously a complete and hardened criminal, so any speech to him is a waste of time.'

Henley is currently spending his time in an Illinois super-maximum-security prison alongside teflon don John Gotti and the rest of America's most wanted. He spends twenty-three hours a day in his cell and becomes eligible for parole in 2031, when he reaches 65.

LARS ELSTRUP

The wildest goose of 'em all

After winning the European Championship in 1992 with Denmark in one of sport's great fairytales, the prodigiously talented Luton Town footballer quit the beautiful game at the height of his powers to join the Wild Geese religious commune in Copenhagen. During his time with the Geese, he was to become 'a body artist' and rechristen himself Dorando, but it was all to end in tears.

Seven years after joining the cult, which he eventually came to run with his then girlfriend, Elstrup decided he needed a dose of self-diagnosed therapy and got it by playing music so loud that it blew all of his speakers. Even hippies draw the line somewhere, and by way of punishment Elstrup's better half denied him visiting rights to his pet daschund. Naturally enough, this was the cue for the suicide bid which saw him kicked out of the commune seven years after he'd joined. 'I was so depressed that I saw no reason to carry on. I tried to hang myself and cut my wrists but I couldn't go through with it. I lay in bed for eighteen hours a day for two years.'

Not that that was the end of loony Lars. He made a brief comeback with Danish side Odense, during which he starred in a memorable testimonial match with former

Denmark keeper Peter Schmeichel. 'He screamed at me to defend,' said Elstrup, 'so I said, "Shut up, you big fuck". He was so shocked he dropped the ball and their striker scored!'

After quitting Odense, Elstrup was soon in trouble again, this time for slapping a schoolboy. And then, nine years after he'd quit football, he mysteriously turned up in the middle of Copenhagen's busiest pedestrian shopping street circled by a rope and waving his penis at passers-by. 'In some respects,' he said shortly before being removed by the police while kicking and screaming and threatening legal action in the European Court of Human Rights, 'I do this to provoke people. I am very aware of people's reactions and I love the fact that people recognise me as Lars Elstrup.'

Nakedness and cross-dressing have become themes for Elstrup. The former striker now wears women's clothing all the time, and was arrested for showing his manhood in a mall while wearing a dress and rollerskates. Asked what he was doing by the police, he said simply: 'We must drop our masks and examine our own shit.'

The last sighting of Elstrup was in London, when he made a guest appearance for the *New Musical Express*'s football side wearing only a pair of skimpy paisley underpants. Having scored five goals in their 9–5 win over lad's mag *Loaded*, during which he had constantly exhorted his team-mates to drink more water, he then ran to the sidelines screaming 'Yellow piss is for losers'. Asked if he fancied a post-match pint, a virtually naked Elstrup answered: 'No . . . pussy' and was last seen running full-tilt towards the fleshpots of Soho.

RAE CARRUTH

Happy families? Not him . . .

The man with a head shaped like a baked bean rivals Darryl Henley and OJ Simpson for first place in the gridiron Hall of Shame, which is quite some boast. A real up-and-comer for the Carolina Panthers NFL team, his gravy train hit the buffers in 1999 when his 24-year-old girlfriend Cherica Adams told him she was expecting his child. Not wanting to play happy families and with hefty drugs debts to service, the thought of handing over any of his $650,000 salary in child maintenance payments was quickly dismissed as a non-starter. The solution? The little Rae of sunshine coldly arranged for a heavily pregnant Adams to be the victim of a drive-by killing in which she was shot four times in November 1999.

He hired Van Brett Watkins to do the actual shooting, and under questioning, he soon confessed. Both Watkins and his friend Michael Kennedy, who drove the car that carried Watkins, gave identical testimony – and both of them put Carruth squarely in the frame as the mastermind of the plot. The most damning evidence of all, however, came from the mouth of the dying mother-to-be. In obvious pain, Adams told the operator who fielded her 911 call that Carruth had pulled his Ford Expedition in front of her car, forcing her to stop, before 'somebody pulled up beside me and did this. I think he [Carruth] did it. I don't know what to think.'

It didn't look good when the FBI, searching for Carruth, tracked him down in a motel parking lot, where they found him in the trunk of a Toyota surrounded by candy bar wrappers and a bottle of his own urine. He'd been there for almost twenty-four hours, curled up in the foetal position.

In the face of strong evidence, further notes written by Adams before she died, and unflattering testimony from two ex-girlfriends, Carruth put up a flimsy defence. In a version of events contradicted by just about every other witness, he maintained that an angry Watkins shot Adams on his own because Adams had made an obscene gesture at him from her car after he had earlier rowed with Carruth because the gridiron star had backed out of a drug deal. It cut little ice. As a nation watched transfixed, it was clear to everyone that it was an embarrassingly porous yarn. Although Carruth's lawyers managed to get him off the death penalty that would have accompanied the first-degree murder conviction sought by prosecutors, there was little doubt about his guilt, and his lack of remorse or emotion did little to endear him to judge or jury.

Convicted of conspiracy to commit murder, of shooting into an occupied vehicle and of using a gun with intent to kill an unborn child, Carruth will be behind bars until approximately 2039. That's if he lives that long: the numbskull has already had two spells in solitary confinement in Raleigh's maximum security jail for his own safety after fighting with other inmates.

His son Chancellor, however, was successfully delivered by emergency Caesarian section, but still bears the legacy of his traumatic entry to the world. Despite being a very rich child, he suffers from cerebral palsy and was unable to walk, hold a bottle or spoon until he was three years of age.

MICKEY THOMAS

Cheeky chappie from the Valleys

Mickey Thomas was always a bit of a jack the lad, even to the point that for several seasons *Match of the Day*'s opening sequence included the bit of footage that had him smiling and winking to the camera after conning his way to a highly dubious free-kick. A gifted winger who could even run rings around Tommy Docherty, he gave a hint of the cheeky cockiness which was later to land him in deep water when Chelsea chairman Ken Bates came calling.

In 1978 Bates was desperate to sign the mercurial Welshman who was then playing for Wrexham and travelled all the way up to Wales, only to find that Thomas – who had an urgent appointment at the local bookies – was a no-show. Undeterred, Bates set up another meeting. This time Thomas turned up on the dot of 10am. Bates, determined to gain a measure of revenge for the Welshman's earlier extraction of urine, didn't. Thomas had the last laugh, though: when Chelsea eventually signed him six years later, it was on condition that he moved closer to London. Thomas did: he decamped ten miles down the road, moving from Colwyn Bay to Rhyl. It's staggering that he lasted seven years in Chelsea's colours.

By the early 1990s, Thomas was still able to raise his game for the odd last hurrah, such as when his wonderful free-kick famously helped Fourth Division Wrexham to knock champions Arsenal out of the FA Cup, but it was for his off-field antics that he was soon to become most famous. The 'Welsh George Best' lived up to that moniker in 1992 when Rhyl's classiest geezer found himself down a country lane shagging his brother-in-law's wife in the

back of a car. Needless to say, the brother-in-law took a pretty dim view of proceedings and, catching the pair in *flagrante delicto*, plunged a screwdriver into Thomas's backside. He then dragged the former footballing genius into the road, where he administered a going-over even more thorough than the one his wife had just received. Thomas was in hospital for a week.

It only took the Welshman a year to comfortably eclipse the notoriety gained in that incident, however. In 1993 he was caught passing dud £10 and £20 notes to the trainees at Wrexham and sentenced to eighteen months in prison. Judge Gareth Edwards told him that he had 'an image of himself as a flash and daring adventurer' before sending him off to share a cell in Liverpool's Walton Jail with a big bloke in dungarees who admitted on Day One that he was incarcerated for beheading his victims.

But the cheeky Welshman still got the last laugh, earning a living as an after-dinner speaker whose favourite gag remains 'They say that Roy Keane's on fifty grand a week. Well, so I was I until they found my presses.'

MARV ALBERT

Baddest granddaddy of 'em all

Squeaky-clean NBC sports pundit Marv Albert's popularity took a dive in 1997 when America's favourite grandfather was charged with sexual assault and battery. He was alleged to have repeatedly bitten former girlfriend Vanessa Perhach on her bum and back (he broke the skin in twelve places) before forcing her to perform oral sex on him and forcibly buggering her. Marv initially denied the charges, but when he offered a plea-bargain and copped a guilty verdict on the charge of misdemeanour assault charges, his ratings went below zero.

Worse was to follow in 1998 when, during investigations into the murder of 58-year-old dominatrix Nadia Frey, police found Albert's name and number among her possessions, though there is no suggestion that he was connected to her murder. Frey specialised in 'restraining, spanking and daipering men', and bad penny Perhach quickly popped up to allege that she and Marv had had three-way sex with New York's most popular dominatrix, who also went under the name of Mistress Hilda.

Marv denied Perhach's colourful assertions and although his career never quite hit the same level as it had before he was fired by NBC in 1997 after he pleaded guilty for assault on Perhach, he was allowed back at the station by 1999.

Marv is by no means the only commentator to run foul of his employers though. There have been plenty of other sports television presenters to have come a cropper Stateside, with Dallas Cowboys great, turned television pundit, Michael Irvin being one famous example of a man who gave his squeaky clean American network a dilemma when he was charged with cocaine and marijuana possession.

Things aren't much different across the Pond. David Icke may have dominated the loony English TV presenters' competition, but iconic English football commentators Frank Bough and Gerald Sinstadt did their best to hold their ends up, as it were. In 1989, the smooth-talking, jumper-wearing Bough was exposed by a national newspaper as a serial swinger who spiced up life with a few lines of coke while watching sex parties with his hookers. The 71-year-old was sacked by the BBC, but started to rebuild his television career in the independent sector. That all ended in 1992 when Bough was caught visiting a Miss Whiplash sex den. That was over and out, thanks Frank.

Even more disturbing – and this was akin to finding out that Dickie Davies worships Satan and cuts the heads off black cats in his garden shed – was the day when a 64-year-old Sinstadt was arrested at a hard-core porn cinema and charged with gross indecency. Which was, well, gross. Police later dropped the charge, but the damage was done.

EAMON DUNPHY

Eamon, this is yer life

Although Marv Albert's arse-biting and three-in-a-bed with a dominatrix probably wins him the gold medal for nutty behaviour by a commentator, epic Irish trouble-maker Eamon Dunphy has devoted himself to giving marvellous Marvin a run for his money.

A pugnacious journeyman footballer in his day, the little Dubliner has established himself as the most out-spoken pundit – gobshite in the local vernacular – on the Emerald Isle. From Italia '90 onwards, when Jack Charlton's Ireland football team was becoming the side no other wanted to meet, even famously beating Italy in the USA World Cup in 1994, Dunphy would incense fans by lambasting the national side for its lack of verve at every available opportunity. So vitriolic were his comments on the subject that Charlton would immediately leave a press conference if he arrived. Ireland's football fans showed their anger in an equally unambiguous manner, mobbing his car in a Dublin street and then overturning it.

Still, Dunphy brought a lot on himself. During the 2002 World Cup, with Irish football in the midst of a row caused by his confidant Roy Keane's acrimonious bust-up with manager Mick McCarthy, Dunphy went onto Irish television after another dire result, saying: 'I want Irish soccer to fulfil its destiny. I want us to fail. I hoped that Cameroon would beat us, that Germany would beat us, and that we would go out of this tournament.'

He managed to survive the outcry over that little outburst, but he soon put his employers in an even more difficult situation. Neither the public nor the controllers of RTE, the Irish equivalent of the BBC, could believe it when Dunphy then turned up to commentate on the Japan–Russia game having had no sleep and with drink clearly taken. After stumbling through a couple of inanities at the start of the match and making no contribution while slumped in his chair, Dunphy slurred his way through the half-time analysis, and did not appear for the second half. Overwhelmed by 1,300 complaints, RTE sacked him on the spot.

Not that Dunphy reserves his ire for sportsmen or only falls out with fellas who kick a ball for a living. He even managed to become estranged from U2, whose manager, Paul McGuinness, remains one of his faithful drinking partners on his regular excursions to Dublin's Horseshoe Bar and at the city's trendiest nightclub, Lilly's Bordello. Granted unfettered access to the supergroup for the book *Unforgettable Fire: The Definitive Biography of U2*, he failed to produce the expected hagiography, instead turning out a warts 'n' all effort that had so many warts that only The Edge will now acknowledge him. Dunphy's ghost-written autobiography of Keane was similarly incendiary: so lurid in fact, that Keane actually denied having made some of the most contentious revelations.

His high-profile radio talkback show and his column in a national Sunday newspaper regularly got him into even more hot water. Successfully sued on a ruinously regular basis, his high point came when Proinsias de Rossa, the then leader of the opposition, won a record £300,000 in damages from him.

Amusing one minute, acerbic the next (and often both simultaneously), Dunphy remains one of the highest-profile personalities in Ireland. Part of that is because he's a maverick, part is because he can laugh at himself; when he was arrested for drink driving before getting off on a technicality, he quipped that 'the problem with Dublin is that you can't get good coke in this town'.

H'ANGUS

A cheeky monkey

For most of the week he is a quiet, studious 28-year-old called Stuart Drummond. On Saturday afternoons, however, the 6ft 4in football fanatic from the North East of England becomes a raging ball of furry testosterone which goes by the name of H'Angus and which has brought controversy to the hitherto noble art of being a football mascot.

Drummond's weekend persona as a Hartlepool Town-supporting ape was inspired by the 'monkey-hangers' nickname given to the folk of his hometown, Hartlepool, by the people of neighbouring towns. The sneering reference to the stupidity of Hartlepool's inhabitants dates from the Napoleonic Wars, during which a French ship sank off the town. The only survivor from the shipwreck was a monkey which, not altogether surprisingly, couldn't answer the questions fired at it by the suspicious

townsfolk – so they promptly hanged it as a French spy.

Since then, H'Angus has been doing his level best to prove stupidity and mayhem are still alive and well in Hartlepool. And he chooses Saturday afternoons to make his point.

The unruly mascot of Hartlepool United is regularly in trouble, mainly for assaulting other mascots – he was famously sent off for grabbing a Gladiator mascot's privates. Other antics include being sent off for chasing a group of pom-pom girls during a game against Barnet, being sent to the stand for dropping his shorts at York, being sent to the stand for taking a corner at Darlington, being sent to the stand for smashing a guitar on the goalpost in imitation of The Who's Pete Townshend, and being sent to the stand for spraying water over the opposition dugout.

However, H'Angus's most shameful episode came when, just six months after facing the sack after being arrested for simulating sex with a pretty (and pretty fed up) female steward in front of 5,000 baying fans at Scunthorpe's Glanford Park, the monkey arrived at Blackpool's Bloomfield Road drunk and carrying a blow-up doll. He then started a fight with two ten-year-old boys before being arrested (again) and ejected from the ground. The club managed to see the funny side though. After releasing him with a reprimand, a club spokesman said: 'he is a cheeky monkey, after all'.

Rather than find his antics embarrassing, the good folk of Hartlepool are so proud of H'Angus that, when he entered the contest to be elected as mayor of Hartlepool, he won by a landslide. Not only that, but after administering an annual budget of £150m for four years, he was then re-elected by a similarly huge margin. Of course, he did the job as Stuart Drummond. The only downside for club supporters is that his official role means he no longer has the time to don the monkey outfit on Saturdays. As avid Hartlepool fan Robin Meredith, 40, said: 'He's a lunatic. But when the football's bad – which is often – H'Angus entertains us. He'll be sorely missed but he's got a more important role now.'

Drummond has promised to return to Hartlepool Town FC when his political career draws to a close, but he has already started a trend for bad behaviour on the sidelines. Swansea's mascot Cyril the Swan was hauled in front of the FA for attacking Norwich City manager Gary Megson. The 9ft bird was also in trouble two weeks later during Millwall's visit to Vetch Field, when he drop-kicked rival mascot Zampa The Lion's head into the crowd; he was once fined £1,000 by magistrates for chucking a pork pie at West Ham fans. Cyril's party piece is abseiling down the floodlighting pylons before games.

Mascot madness has taken harmless forms, such as Robbie the Bobby, the mascot at Bury, who was arrested for mooning at rival fans, and Halifax Town's Freddie the Fox, who was ejected from the Rochdale ground after he cocked a leg on the opposition's goalpost and sparked a riot. But it has also resulted in its fair share of punch-ups: Wolfie, the Wolverhampton Wanderers' lucky charmer, emerged unscathed from a fight with West Bromwich Albion's Baggie the Bird, and was doing quite well against Bristol City's junior mascots the Three Little Pigs, but got the mother and father of kickings when the Bristol City Cat weighed in.

However, perhaps the saddest mascot nuttiness occurred in 2002 when Freddie the Fox, the winner of the annual Mascot Grand National at Huntingdon – a once-yearly spot of fun designed chiefly to raise money for charity – was unmasked as Olympic 400-metre semi-finalist Matthew Douglas and promptly disqualified.

MARGE SCHOTT

Major League racist

Baseball fans in Cincinnati loved Reds' owner Marge Schott, even if they were genuinely divided on the key question: was she a racist bitch or simply a misguided, eccentric little old lady? The evidence, it has to be said, points to the former.

A noted philanthropist and animal lover who took control of the Cincinnati Reds in December 1984, Marge was prone to engaging her mouth before she'd got her brain in gear. Her most famous faux pas came during an interview with the *New York Times* in 1992, in which Marge – a German-American (nee Unnewehr) with a size-able collection of Nazi memorabilia – said that: 'Hitler did some pretty good things before he went nuts'. That brought her a $250,000 fine from Major League commissioner Bud Selig, plus a year's ban from games, a punishment which was levied again in 1996 when she stood up for Adolf once again.

Just to show she was inclusively offensive, the profane former second-hand car dealer also had her say on Asians. First she complained that 'I don't like it when high school-aged Asian Americans come here and stay so long and then outdo our kids. That's not right.' Then she claimed that she didn't know why the use of the word 'Japs' was regarded as offensive. On another occasion she spoke in a mock Japanese accent while recalling a meeting with the Japanese prime minister. In 1994, she outraged the city's gay community when she banned her players from wearing earrings because 'only fruits wear earrings'.

Her attitude to her black players was even more worrying. She referred to 'Martin Luther King Day' as 'Nigger Day' and then claimed her use of the word 'nigger' was

'a joke'. In 1991 team controller Tim Sabo sued Schott, saying she fired him because he opposed her policy of not hiring blacks, alleging that Schott called black outfielders Eric Davis and Dave Parker 'my million-dollar niggers'. Marge issued a statement denying that she was a racist, but later that month another executive, Sharon Jones, quoted Marge as saying she would 'never hire another nigger. I'd rather have a trained monkey working for me than a nigger.'

If Marge wasn't overly fond of black people, Asians, or gays, she did, however, love animals. She enjoyed a successful career breeding thoroughbreds and once turned up at a fund-raiser party at Cincinnati's exclusive Queen City Club with a live dancing bear as her escort.

She also lavished her affections on Schottzie, her 15-stone St Bernard. So pampered was Schottzie that he accompanied Marge to the announcement that she'd bought her hometown team in 1984. Despite being an unfeasibly smelly heap of dogflesh, the mutt was in every team photo during Marge's seventeen-year reign, always wearing a Reds cap. He even had his own seat next to Marge for home games, and she'd parade him around the infield and rub his fur against her players – a practice that the MLB, with whom she was in a state of continual warfare, eventually ordered her to stop after numerous complaints from Reds players.

Marge was unrepentant, though. 'Pets are always there

for you,' said Marge in 1991 when she announced Schottzie's passing. 'They never ask for anything. They never ask for a raise. They're very special.'

For all the money she gave to charity, there's little doubt that Marge could be a tad selfish and a little tight. She refused to give left fielder Eric Davis a plane ticket home after he was hospitalised with a damaged kidney suffered after attempting a diving catch during the 1990 World Series. And in 1996, when veteran umpire John McSherry had a heart-attack in the outfield during the opening game of the season, forcing the game to be called off, Marge whined on live television: 'Why is this happening to me?' When that led to a wave of complaints she sent the dead man's family a bouquet of flowers – which turned out to have been a recycled bunch sent to her earlier that day by a television company.

TY COBB

'Ty Cobb is a prick'

Ty Cobb, otherwise known as the Georgia Peach, is probably the nastiest bastard on this whole list, and certainly one of the most talented. One of the most sublime baseball batters of all time, the Detroit Tiger was also such a

racist, misogynist, and violent drunk that his hand-picked biographer, Al Stump, later called Cobb 'the most violent, successful, thoroughly maladjusted personality ever to pass across American sports'. Ernest Hemingway was a bit more succinct: he described Cobb as 'a total shit'. Babe Ruth was most succinct of all: 'Ty Cobb is a prick'.

A baseball Hall-of-Famer, Cobb was so utterly unpleasant that despite over twenty years at the top before hanging up his bat in 1928, not one former team-mate turned up at his funeral in 1961. Not that anybody was surprised: he fought with team-mates and opposition alike, spiked fellow players, hit them, screamed at them and once even tried to fight fellow Hall-of-Famer Lou Gehrig, the New York Yankees' peerless (and peerlessly behaved) batsman. So unpleasant was Cobb that when the team played away and travelled by train he insisted upon having his own compartment and slept with a gun under a pillow because he was obsessed with the idea that one of his team-mates would murder him given half a chance. He was probably right to worry.

But if Cobb hated his team-mates, it was as nothing compared to the bile he reserved for the fans. A notorious and open racist, at various stages he stabbed a black groundskeeper, grabbed his wife by the throat, and pushed a black chambermaid down the stairs. In one particularly appalling incident in 1912 at New York City's Hilltop Park, Cobb jumped into the stands and relentlessly battered a fan he said had verbally abused him. Nobody else had heard the fan, who happened to be black *and* handicapped – he had no fingers – say anything untoward.

Nobody was safe from Cobb's psychopathic temper. In 1921, by which time he had become the Tigers' player-manager, he confronted umpire Billy Evans under the stands after a game. After lambasting the poor official, and then telling him that 'I only fight one way, to kill', Cobb went berserk and repeatedly slammed the umpire's head against a slab of concrete until Evans lost consciousness.

As he had already beaten-up several newsmen, the incident was kept under wraps.

A millionaire many times over, Cobb lived in a huge mansion but refused to have it connected to the national grid because he thought the electric companies charged too much for their services.

Given his fondness for wanton violence, his love for filthy lucre, and the fact that he always carried a handgun, it must have been a brave man who'd try to mug him, yet in 1912 someone was stupid enough to attempt to steal Cobb's wallet. The man was, naturally enough, pistol whipped by his intended victim, who then stabbed him to death. Cobb got off on the basis of self-defence, but was soon in trouble again. Later that same year, he was the chief suspect in a murder which took place in broad daylight outside of Boston's Fenway Park. The unfortunate man had been beaten to death with a baseball bat, but despite several witnesses, not one was willing to identify Cobb, who was never charged.

Few sportsmen have been more despicable human beings than Cobb, as Ron Shelton, a former minor league player who wrote and directed the film *Cobb*, which examined the darker sides of the Georgia Peach's life, was the first to admit. 'All the bottled rage he seems to have on the field, the fights, the incidents with fans, the social dysfunction – that's all Cobb,' said Shelton.

The man himself was utterly unrepentant though.

'They were all against me, tried every trick to cut me down,' said Cobb shortly before he died. 'But I beat the bastards and left them in the ditch.'

UDAY HUSSEIN

Football manager from hell

At the height of the fight against apartheid, Nelson Mandela memorably declared that: 'Sport can never be normal in an abnormal society'. Thousands of miles away in Iraq, a psychopath named Uday Hussein, son of Saddam, was energetically proving him right – jailing, torturing, and killing underperforming athletes. According to Issam Thamer al-Diwan, who played volleyball for Iraq between 1974 and 1987 before defecting, 'dozens of athletes and leaders in the Iraqi sports movement' had been executed because 'Uday cannot stand to think that someone in Iraq could be smarter or more famous than him'.

Rumours of football players having the soles of their feet whipped with piano wire had done the rounds, with FIFA, world football's governing body, sending two investigators to Baghdad in 1997 to question members of the Iraqi national team who had allegedly had their feet caned by Uday's henchmen after losing a World Cup qualifying match to Kazakhstan. Needless to say, none of the players were keen to talk about the episode.

If was only after the fall of Saddam's Ba'athist regime that the excesses of Uday could be fully chronicled. The first piece of evidence came when the building housing the Iraqi Football Association was overrun. Inside, American troops found a sarcophagus-shaped 'iron maiden'. Over seven-feet high, three-feet wide and deep enough to house a man, the device had long spikes fixed to the inside of the door so the victim was impaled as it closed. The spikes were blunt from use.

Virtually all of the violence in Iraqi sport was instigated by Uday, and he'd often mete out punishments himself. A man who didn't let his lack of prowess stand in his way as a player – he was selected for Iraq on several occasions – he was also the manager from hell. Midfielder Saad Keis Naoman was unlucky to be playing in a side managed by Uday when he was red-carded for questioning the referee's parentage. Unimpressed, Uday decided to teach Naoman a lesson and sentenced him to a month in the infamous al-Radwaniya jail, where he was beaten daily on his back with a wooden cane until he lost consciousness. He was then dragged behind a jeep before being submerged in a sewage tank to infect his wounds.

That, with minor variations, was the standard penalty

for incurring Uday's displeasure. 'Every single day I was beaten on my feet, and was not allowed to eat or drink,' said Sharar Haydar, a defender, who went through the first of four spells of imprisonment and torture when Iraq was beaten 2–0 by Jordan in 1993. Soon after he told Uday that he didn't want to play for Iraq against the USA the next year, he was whipped and dragged through filthy water until the cuts became infected. His scariest moment was in the lead-up to the 1994 World Cup in America when, after a series of bravura performances in the qualifiers, Iraq only had to beat lowly Qatar to qualify for the finals. Sitting in the dressing room, a call came through from Saddam's youngest son: 'Uday rang to give us a message: "If you don't win I will kill you".' Unsurprisingly, they lost. Uday had a set system of punishments for mistakes that occur routinely – a defensive error brought three days inside, a missed penalty three weeks – and after three more spells in jail, Haydar fled the country in 1998.

'Uday decided everything, which clubs you played for, everything,' said Haydar. 'You kept your mouth shut or you were killed, but Iraqi fans loved abusing [a club called] al-Rasheed. They couldn't tell Uday what they thought of him so they yelled at his team. Saddam didn't like that, so he shut down the club.'

Uday died during a firefight with American marines in 2004.

TONYA HARDING

Trailer trash on ice

Leading up to the 1994 Winter Olympics in Lillehammer, Norway, ice-skating was so big that the US federation had just signed a ten-year $100m television deal to bring it into the top rank of non-team sports. A major reason for its popularity was the forthcoming confrontation between Tonya Harding and Nancy Kerrigan. For most viewers Stateside the two American ice dancers were virtually assured of the gold and silver medals, it was just a question of which finished first and which came second.

Kerrigan versus Harding was the sort of contest on which America would love to gorge at every Olympics. It was a clash of opposites: Harding, the brash, white trailer trash from Portland, Oregon, versus Kerrigan, the refined Ivy League sorority queen from the American equivalent of the Home Counties. Skating was well-established as one of the blue riband events of the games and with two Yanks ruling the roost, the contest pushed all the right buttons for the public and their networks in the land of the free.

Happy to prevail by fair means or foul, Harding chose the latter. As the then 21-year-old said the year before the Olympics, 'I've had to overcome many obstacles, but

I've never given up hope. I didn't come with a silver spoon in my mouth. I've had to work for what I have. This is for anybody. If you have a dream, go for it. There's always a way to make it come true.' And that way was to cheat. Harding had been beaten regularly by Kerrigan in the run up to the Games and set out to ensure it didn't happen again. She had decided that, one way or another, it would be her face leading the news headlines after the medal ceremony. In that, if in nothing else, she succeeded beyond her wildest dreams.

The incident which would make Harding endure in sporting infamy was caught live on video tape on 6 January 1994 at the US National Trials. Kerrigan was just about to climb onto the ice when a low blur appears from rightfield and the brunette skater goes down, screaming. As onlookers rushed to Kerrigan, who was holding her right knee in agony, a figure makes a hasty exit. Quickly apprehended, he was identified as Shane Stant.

The conspiracy began to unravel at once. Stant, along with his uncle-cum-getaway-driver Derrick Smith, 'body-guard' Shawn Ekert, and Harding's on-off husband Jeff Gillooly, formed a none-too-bright four-strong team of conspirators who aimed to put Kerrigan out of action ahead of the Olympics in the next month. In that they failed as the injury sustained by Kerrigan from the assault was relatively minor. Initially kicked off the US team,

Harding threatened a $25m lawsuit and made the plane to Norway amid fevered media interest.

In the event, neither skater won gold – that honour went to unsung Oksana Baiul of Ukraine – but the long arm of the law soon caught up with Harding. Gillooly got two years, with the other conspirators getting eighteen months each and the judge roundly condemning them as 'greedy, dishonest, even stupid'. Although the hatchet-faced caravan-dweller continued to insist that she was innocent of all charges m'lud, that quickly wore thin; she changed her plea to guilty to conspiracy to hinder prosecution in an attack on Kerrigan, copping three years' probation, $160,000 in fines, and 500 hours of community service.

Banned for life from skating for the USA, Harding has tried various means of scraping a living. There was topless ice skating in Vegas, appearing as a skating Santa Claus, minor league ice hockey, a walk on role in the low-budget movie *Breakaway*, a boxing career that saw her appear on a Mike Tyson undercard, wrestling in Japan, and even an abortive attempt to skate for Norway or Sweden. ('With her blonde hair and blue eyes, she looks Norwegian or Swedish,' said agent David Hans Schmidt. 'My client would still like to win the gold medal she never got. If it has to be as a Norwegian or Bolivian, that's fine with us.')

But mainly there was trouble. She was arrested for

throwing a hubcap at her live-in boyfriend before repeatedly punching him in the face, leaving him needing hospital treatment. She even claimed to have been abducted at knifepoint outside her home by a 'bushy-haired stranger', although no one was ever arrested.

VINCE COLEMAN

Light the blue touch paper

What do you do if you're a 32-year-old baseball player earning $3m a year when you've seen better days and you're playing for a club whose fans think you're one of the laziest no-goods ever to pull on their famous shirt? Simple: you give them a cast iron excuse to fire you.

That's exactly what former New York Mets batsman Vince Coleman did before he was unceremoniously turfed out of the Big Apple. Just for good measure, Coleman made sure he got successfully sued by a two-year-old fan.

Coleman had already been in bother at the Mets before that fateful day at Los Angeles' Dodgers Stadium in July 1993. Despite claiming to be 'a loving, caring, sharing guy who wants the best for everybody', there had been the incidents where he had taken a four-iron to the Mets' star pitcher Doc Gooden, the confrontation with coach Mike Cubbage in his first year at the Mets and the rape charges in Florida (later dropped when prosecutors decided the victim's testimony did not hold up).

But the *coup de grâce* came when the team was playing in Los Angeles and Coleman hooked up with an old friend, Eric Davies, and two other Dodgers players. Screeching around the stadium in Davies' Jeep Cherokee with the music up and the windows down, Coleman was leaning out of the window when he realized that he 'just happened' to have a couple of firecrackers in his pocket 'left over from Thanksgiving'.

Spotting a crowd of autograph hunters huddled together waiting by the back entrance to the ground in the players' parking lot, Coleman decided the best thing would be to announce his arrival in grand style. So he lobbed a couple of the little explosives in the direction of the waiting fans before fleeing the site giggling maniacally. Unfortunately, although the court was later to hear that the incendiary devices only cost $1.50 each, they weren't run-of-the-mill firecrackers, but bangers described on the packaging as an 'M-100 explosive device'.

By the time two-year-old Amanda Santos, 11-year-old Marshall Savoy, and 33-year-old Cindy Mayhew reached hospital, they had sustained second-degree burns to cheek and damage to an eye and finger; a badly bruised leg; and an acute ear injury. Coleman, who later pleaded guilty to a misdemeanour charge of possessing an explosive device, and received a one-year suspended jail sentence, three years' probation, a $1,000 fine, and 200 hours of community service, was diagnosed as having a missing brain. He was also missing a good chunk of money after settling out of court, and his job went AWOL – the New York Mets fired him on the spot.

Coleman blamed the New York media for demonising him, saying that he was merely following his team-mates' lead. In a move calculated to win friends in the dressing room, he said: 'Look at [pitcher] Bret Saberhagen. He shot bleach on reporters on purpose. He threw firecrackers at reporters intentionally.' Just for good measure, he acted as his own character witness. 'I'm a good guy. I've been misconstrued. I think it's been blown out of proportion. I just thought it was a joke. We were just having fun.'

JOHN LAMBIE

'Tell him he's Pele'

A long-term manager of Glasgow's 'other' side, Partick Thistle, John Lambie is a singular man of outrageous contrasts and mind-boggling inconsistencies. He's a born-again Christian who brings a chaplain into the dressing room before matches and then goes on to deliver pre-match tirades with a 'fuck' quotient that would have Peter Reid scurrying for cover. He's a die-hard Rangers fan who is a living legend at a club which has a rejection of the Old Firm and their sectarian attitudes at its core value. He's a renowned disciplinarian who hands out more fines in an average week than the Strathclyde constabulary's motorised division, yet is a father figure who once served his players champagne before they went out to play Rangers at Firhill in 1992 (beating them 3–0).

Lambie is defined by the unique sense of humour, one which saw Partick become a haven for loonies of every hue during his tenure. His ready wit is legendary, but there's one story which beats all the others. It dates from the day when striker Colin McGlashan was involved in a clash of heads and emerged from the Firhill turf dazed and confused. Told by the physio that McGlashan had concussion and didn't know who he was, Lambie replied: 'Great. Rattle that sponge about his face, tell him he's fucking Pele and get him back on the field.'

Lambie comes from the hard former mining town of Whitburn, in the heart of the area known as Wild West Lothian. Hewn from the same background as men like Matt Busby and Bill Shankly, he qualifies as a true berserker mainly because of his penchant for signing players with (at best) questionable approaches to discipline. 'Former Clydebank chairman Jack Steedman says that

John Lambie

whenever he wonders where all the nutters in Scottish football have gone, that he looks at Partick Thistle and realizes I have them all under my roof,' said Lambie in the mid-'90s. 'There would be nothing worse than goody-goody players sitting in the dressing room like dummies. That's not my way. Guys like Chic Charnley, Albert Craig, Allan Dinnie, and Don McVicar kept me alive. They had that bit of badness about them that all winners must have in their make-up.'

It's no surprise that Lambie should mention Charnley in particular. In an episode as famous as Lambie's Pele outburst, Charnley (who was sent off a record seventeen times in his career) secured his status as Scottish football's premier league nutcase during a training session at Ruchill Public Park off Glasgow's Maryhill Road, an area which is very much in the wrong part of town. Halfway through the warm-up, two samurai sword-wielding hooligans invaded the park intent upon sorting out the Partick players. In one of the most chilling manoeuvres since the Charge of the Light Brigade, Charnley rushed headlong at them, armed with nothing but a bad attitude, dodgy tattoos, a row of missing teeth, and a traffic cone, seeing the interlopers off before insisting the session was restarted. The legend of Lambie's crazy gang was complete.

A compulsive gambler in his youth ('if I won at the horses, I was away to the dogs at night and if I won at the dogs, I was away at the horses next day'), Lambie knows all the tricks. He has levied so many fines that he once took the team for a pre-season break on the back of the previous season's fines. But Lambie does whatever works, no matter how unorthodox. He has left players fighting in the changing room at half-time, employed a club chaplain to talk to the players and drawn inspiration from American self-help guru Joyce Meyer, a regular on Evangelical TV programme Godslot.

After one particularly dismal first-half, fanatical pigeon-fancier Lambie unveiled a revolutionary concoction designed to re-invigorate flagging doos (the Scottish word for pigeons). Under duress, each player swallowed sachets of the rancid brew. It was a placebo, but they won. Nobody fancied taking the stuff the next week. Then there was the attention-grabbing episode when Lambie became celibate in protest at the team's limp form. Only when they started scoring did Mrs Lambie start smiling again. Lambie had a bulldog poster on his door which said simply 'Piss Off'. No wonder his players thought the sun shone out of him.

MIKE DANTON

Love–hate lunacy

The circumstances in which NHL (National Hockey League) star Mike Danton was sentenced to seven-and-a-half years in prison for trying to have his agent killed are bizarre in the extreme. In fact, so twisted is the Canadian ice hockey forward's relationship with David Frost, the agent and mentor who Danton paid $10,000 to have assassinated, that the truth may never really be known. 'I do not believe in over 18 years on the bench I have been faced with a case as bizarre as this one,' said federal Judge William D. Stiehl.

Danton first met Frost as a ten-year-old, while the coach was 25, and over the years the two hockey-obsessives formed an unnaturally close bond. Eventually, the teenage player, alienated and estranged from his parents, was persuaded by Frost to move out of his parents' house and move in with Frost and three other promising young players in what the court later heard was a cult-like atmosphere. Frost even persuaded the player to change his name from that of his parents, Jefferson, to Danton, which was the name of a kid at hockey camp. Frost, who was under police investigation for the sexual exploitation of three 16- and 17-year-old girls and would later come under investigation for punching one of his players while he was on the bench for an NHL side, had already banned Danton from hugging his parents after matches, and Danton now cut off all contact with his worried mother and father.

Eventually, Danton began to spread his wings and, by the time he established himself as a forward for the St Louis Blues, Frost was struggling to maintain control of a player who was gorging on booze and groupies. In an effort to keep his grip, Frost put pressure on Danton to pay back $25,000 he owed his agent (ie Frost), implying that he would tell the Blues about Danton's promiscuity, his mis-use of painkillers and sleeping pills, plus his drink-problem, if he didn't. That's when Danton, never the most stable of souls, snapped.

Using his unwitting 19-year-old girlfriend Katie Wolfmeyer as a go-between, Danton offered a would-be hit man $10,000 to remove Frost from the face of the earth. Only later, after hit man Justin Jones went to the police – not too difficult as he was a police dispatcher – did it emerge that Danton had already tried to hire an assassin on two previous occasions. After initially pretending that he only wanted to have Frost beaten up, Danton came clean and admitted his guilt.

The really spooky bit came during the trial when Frost, despite overwhelming evidence, continued to deny that he was the intended target of the hit man. 'I know for a fact it wasn't me. It was a hit man. He hired a hit man because he thought a hit man was coming to get him.' Even spookier was the fact that Frost had to be barred from talking to Danton, so assiduously was the svengali trying to coach his young charge to engineer a plea of diminished responsibility. If someone had tried to have you killed three times, would you help them get off the murder rap?

Danton still hasn't changed his name back and refuses to speak to his parents or answer their letters. He is, though, still in the throes of a truly bizarre love-hate relationship with his mentor Frost.

JACK JOHNSON

Mister unconventional

Context is everything, and while the vast majority of today's heavyweight boxers are black and bling, when Jack Johnson was growing up at the turn of last century, being loud and proud was a life-threatening state of mind. That was true in all of America, but was especially the case in the Deep South in Galveston, Texas when Johnson, the son of a sharecropper, was growing up.

Yet Johnson was never one to be restrained by conven-

Jack Johnson

tion. Having come up through the Battle Royals – where young blacks would fight pell-mell while whites watched – Johnson was old beyond his years. After he was arrested in 1903 (boxing was technically illegal in Texas and mixed-race boxing was definitely illegal across the whole of the south) he moved to Chicago and by 1907 he defeated former world champion Bob Fitzsimmons before going on to beat Canadian world champion Tommy Burns the next year.

However, the outrageous behaviour of the first black heavyweight of the world ensured that there wouldn't be another for almost twenty-five years. Jack Johnson managed to offend every section of contemporary white American society, and many parts of black America weren't exactly bursting with pride. As if it wasn't bad enough that he showed no deference to whites or white society, Johnson had three wives, all of them white, and consorted openly with white prostitutes. When his first wife, nightclub owner Etta Duryea, blew her brains out, Johnson was already having an affair with another white woman, Lucille Cameron, whom he married shortly afterwards.

Johnson was clearly enjoying thumbing his nose at the social conventions of the time. One of his favourite tricks, for example, was to wind several feet of bandages around his member before going out to spar in tight shorts, which made him look absurdly well-hung. Almost as bad, he gloated about his victories and taunted his white opponents – white boxers did it all the time, but it was unheard of from a black man.

White society was appalled, and called for Johnson's head. James J. Jeffries, who had never been knocked down in an illustrious career, was brought out of retirement to be the original Great White Hope, but when Johnson beat him in front of 22,000 spectators in Reno, Nevada, on American Independence Day in 1910, race riots erupted in thirty-nine cities across America, with more than a dozen people losing their lives in the process. Footage of Johnson winning was banned in virtually every southern state, including Texas, on the grounds of public safety.

Unable to beat him in the ring, White America pursued him out of it, invoking an obscure piece of legislation called the Mann Act, which was supposed to combat vice. When former girlfriend Belle Schreiber was forced to testify that Johnson had moved Cameron across state borders for immoral purposes, he was sentenced to a year and a day in prison for an offence that was usually treated as a minor misdemeanour. Johnson, reasonably fearing he wouldn't last such a sentence, promptly fled the country.

A bloated and out-of-condition 37-year-old, he eventually lost his title to Kansan Jess Willard in 1915, losing in forty-five rounds in Havana.

ERIC CANTONA

Kung fu fighter

Gav, a misguided mate of mine who's a Manchester United supporter, has a picture of Eric Cantona on his wall. It's not a usual pose for a star of the beautiful game, though. The Frenchman isn't exactly laid-back, although he *is* horizontal – he's hurtling through the air kung fu style towards a Crystal Palace fan who has had the audacity to badmouth him from the stands. The fans in the photograph are slack-jawed and wide-eyed, waiting for the moment when the budding martial artist will connect with the fan's chest. Taken in 1995, it remains the most famous picture in English football since Gazza cried at the 1990 World Cup.

For that assault at Selhurst Park Cantona was banned for eight months and given 120 hours of community service. (When asked to explain why he did it, he told the assembled journalists that 'When the seagulls . . . follow the trawler . . . it's because they think . . . sardines will be thrown . . . into the sea'). But at least he didn't retire (again) after Alex Ferguson talked him out of it. For observers of the self-proclaimed gifted one, that at least was a major surprise because by that stage Eric already had a well-worn track record of spitting the dummy.

In fact, if he hadn't retired from football in his native France at the tender age of 24, he would never have been at Selhurst Park on that damp night in south London. The French weren't remotely surprised by his antics. After all, this was the same Cantona who went on television in August 1988 to call Henri Michel, the then manager of the French national side, a 'shit bag' (actually 'un sac de merde') and was promptly banned. He was sacked by Marseille for throwing his shirt to the ground after being substituted during a match against Torpedo Moscow, and then fined and suspended for fighting with Montpellier team-mate Jean-Claude Lemoult. Finally, he was banned for three matches for throwing the ball at the referee while captaining Nimes. When he shouted 'idiots' (best said in a very Freeeench accent) in the face of each of the three members of the disciplinary panel at the French FA from twlece inches or so, they doubled his ban to two months. Cue Eric's first retirement in December 1991.

So when his trawler hit rocky seas across the Channel, no one was too surprised. After helping Sheffield Wednesday to the first division title and then doing the same in the Premiership with Leeds United, Cantona moved to the club Leeds fans hate above all others, Manchester United. (The move came amid scurrilous but untrue rumours that Cantona had been too friendly with a team-mate's wife at Elland Road, hence the cry from

Manchester United fans when Leeds came to Old Trafford: 'He's French/He's Flash/He's been up Leslie Ash/Cantona! Cantona!', a reference to the other half of Leeds' star centre-forward). Even there, under the nose of the disciplinarian Ferguson, he managed to skirt close to the wind, particularly in Istanbul in 1993 when he took on Istanbul's baton-wielding riot police single-handedly after one of them cracked him over the head as he walked from the pitch having been sent-off.

Cantona does, however, have a more thoughtful side. Well, he'd like to have. At the height of his popularity, he published an impenetrable autobiographical tome, of which the following is the most lucid excerpt: 'When I see them, these boys from Manchester, when they touch me, when they speak to me in hushed voices, I want them to go away happy and convinced that they have met a player who is more like them than they know.' Cantona is now an actor.

DICK CONWAY

Putting his body on the line

Most Kiwis say that they would give their right arm to play for the All Blacks, but few actually get to demonstrate that they would sacrifice a significant part of their anatomy in order to prove themselves worthy of wearing the silver fern. Not so Dick Conway, New Zealand rugby's red wrecker.

A teak tough back-row with copper-red hair who was universally known by the nickname 'Red', Conway made his debut against the 1959 British Lions side, an outfit who they saw off in particularly no-nonsense fashion, winning three matches in gruelling style and drawing one. Conway and Co. dismantled the powder-puff Lions forwards easily.

Having gone through that baptism of fire, it was ironic that it was while playing with his children that summer shortly after the Lions had scuttled home with their tails between their legs that Conway broke his finger during a game of, er, softball. The prognosis was not optimistic: the finger was broken so badly that even when it knitted together there was every prospect that it would break again under the slightest provocation.

Having grafted for much of his life to become an All

Black, Conway wasn't going to let it all slip just when he'd reached the pinnacle of his rugby career, and especially not when the All Blacks were just about to embark on a tour of South Africa – if the Lions were the great northern hemisphere challenge, it was the Springboks who were the Kiwis' real rivals. Nevertheless, the medical opinion was that if he played the sort of no-holds barred rugby that was likely to be seen on the High Veldt (where his finger would surely have been targeted) it would be broken and he would miss the rest of the tour, and probably the Test matches.

The only solution, said his doctor, was to give up the game. Unless, he added as an afterthought, Conway wanted him to whip it off. The words were delivered with a chuckle, but the laughter soon fell flat when Red turned up at the surgery the very next morning and instructed the doc to amputate the dodgy digit. The nine-fingered No.8 duly toured, wearing a protective leather glove.

Not that Conway was the only All Black willing to break the pain barrier to represent his country. Ten years later, Colin Meads – the hardest of them all – played against South Africa with an arm that had been snapped in two at the bottom of a ruck a fortnight before, but was then protected by a soft leather sleeve. He was targeted mercilessly, but gave better than he got.

All Blacks captain Buck Shelford wasn't far behind Meads in the toughness stakes. He didn't lose an arm or a finger, but his injury was arguably worse. His defining moment came in Nantes in 1990, when the All Blacks were about to lose their five-year unbeaten record to an adrenaline-pumped French side. In a match of sustained savagery, Shelford was raked in the nuts, sustaining a ruptured testicle and a cut to his scrotum that later needed eighteen stitches. Three members of the coaching staff had to physically restrain him from going back on and finishing the game (and the French).

Although Conway, Meads and Shelford are all Kiwis, it wouldn't be fair to finish this entry without making some mention of another crazy man who was willing to lose a digit in the blinkered pursuit of sporting excellence. Scottish rally driver Colin McRae – aka 'McCrazy' and 'McCrash' – damaged a finger so badly in the 2002 WRC Rally of Corsica that his participation in the next event, the Rally de Catalunya in Spain, was in doubt. McRae gave doctors permission to remove the finger if it caused him any discomfort during the race. 'People think I'm mad to go for an amputation,' said McRae, 'but if I finish sixth this weekend and win the championship by a single point, then it'll be totally worth it. Winning the world title is worth millions of pounds, so what price a little finger?'

KY LAFFOON

'Drown you bastard, drown'

Ky Laffoon, the talented American golfer and occasional hustler who played during the late Depression and after the war, was 50 per cent Native American and 100 per cent over-emotional. Unlike many of his staid fellow golfers in those buttoned-up times, he wasn't so much a club chucker as a club destroyer. And the club that came in for the most grief was his poor putter.

Legendary American sports writer George Plimpton, in his seminal work *The Bogey Man: An Amateur In Professional Golf*, wrote of the day when he saw Laffoon lose it with the smallest club in the bag when missed putts saw him finish fourth in the 1946 Masters, a tournament he thought he should have won. 'Drown you poor bastard, drown,' shouted Laffoon at the club after he blew yet another putt. He then grabbed his putter by its shaft and shoved it underwater. When Plimpton asked him what he was up to, he said simply: 'It's a private matter between me and the club.'

That wasn't the first or the last time that Laffoon completely lost it with his putter. At one tournament in Arkansas he was so angry that he threw his putter at a tree, only for it to stay wedged up in a branch. So he

Ky Laffoon

threw another club to try to dislodge it, but it also wedged tight. When a third club went the same way, Laffoon left them there: when he came back the next day to retrieve them the hickory was so warped the clubs were unusable. But then Laffoon didn't treat his clubs well: on one round he discarded a club on every hole until, with four to play, he had none left.

His putters bore the brunt of his lunacy. During one tournament in the Florida Keys, Laffoon got so mad that when he missed a short putt on the 18th, he ran to his car, retrieved a pistol and shot the putter three times at close range before getting his caddie to bury the shattered club in a nearby bunker. Tales of him punishing an offending putter by dragging it behind his car – a routine witnessed by team-mate Paul Runyan on a drive between Dallas and Fort Worth – were legion.

Yet Laffoon also liked to give the putter a chance, and on several occasions had to retire from tournaments when he got so angry with his poor putting that he would hit himself on the head with his putter, often hard enough to make him bleed copiously. That streak of self-flagellation wasn't unique to Laffoon; in fact he probably got the idea from a pair of fellow masochists who took their golf way too seriously.

Lefty Stackhouse was another American golfer making a fine living during the Depression, and he was another who regularly drew blood by hitting himself on the head with his putter. He once threw himself into a briar bush after a particularly bad drive and insisted on being left there in his bleeding, self-crucified glory. Another time, after yipping a putt, he plunged his right hand repeatedly into a rose bush until the skin was ripped and bleeding. He looked at his left hand and said: 'And don't think you are getting away with it either,' and plunged it into the bush, repeating the action.

Ivan Gantz, or Ivan The Terrible, was another one of Laffoon's buddies. He once jumped into a cactus after a particularly disappointing tee-shot; another time he just banged his head against a tree until he drew blood. Lots of it. Crazy fellas!

DAMIR DOKIC

Daddy dearest

Pissed, bearded, raging Serbian nutcase Damir Dokic wins the contest for baddest tennis dad of all time by a short head, narrowly beating off some stiff competition. It's close, but his crazed antics at major events are enough to ensure that he collects this particular cigar.

Damir is the former lorry driver and amateur boxer who also happens to be the father of Jelena Dokic, a talented young tennis player who spent much of her youth in Australia, for whom she briefly competed before the Aussie tennis federation (inevitably) fell out with her dad.

So high profile and crazed were Damir's antics that he became almost as famous as his young daughter. In 1999 he was forcibly removed for being drunk and disorderly and for calling officials at Edgbaston Priory Club 'Nazis who supported the bombing of Yugoslavia'. When he lay down in the road, blocking traffic, he was arrested 'for his own safety'. He was up to the same wheezes at Wimbledon the next year, when he abused security staff and refused to leave the grounds, grabbing a journalist's mobile phone and smashing it before running outside, blocking traffic and jumping on the hood of a car before being arrested (again). At the US Open, he made it a hat trick of dismissals when he was ejected from Flushing Meadow for flying into a blind rage over the price of his meal.

Damir eventually fell out with his long-suffering daughter when he accused her of abandoning her family for Brazilian racing driver Enrique Bernoldi (although actually it was the other way round – Jelena's mother divorced him and Jelena banned him from attending matches). 'She left us. I never want to see Jelena again,' he raged. Mind you, it could be worse, she could be a lesbian. 'I will kill myself if Jelena ever becomes a lesbian,' he said. He is no longer part of his daughter's life.

Although there are other challengers for the title of tennis dad from hell – notably the controlling Richard Williams and Steffi Graf's father Peter, an alcoholic former used-car salesman whom the German press called 'Papa Merciless' before he was sentenced to three years and nine months in prison for $4m tax evasion – Dokic's closest rival remains Mary Pierce's French-Canadian clown of a father, Jim.

So offensive was Pierce that not only did the Women's Tennis Association (WTA) ban him from all tour matches, they actually introduced the 'Jim Pierce rule' prohibiting abusive behaviour from players, coaches, and relatives after he punched two fans at the French Open in 1992. 'Mary is like a finely tuned sports car,' said Jim shortly after she had taken out a restraining order preventing him from ever coming near her again. 'I built the Ferrari and now I want the keys back.'

Although not as high profile as the Dokic–Pierce combo, French father Christophe Fauviau has also staked a challenge in the offensive parents category. In 2003, the former Army colonel, whose 12-year-old daughter had been identified as a potential future French Open winner, decided his less talented 16-year-old son Maxime also needed a helping hand. Unfortunately, it all went terribly wrong after a tournament in Dax in southern France. The 43-year-old was arrested for spiking the drinks of Maxime's opponents with an antidepressant drug, Temesta (lorazepam), after

25-year-old Alexandre Lagadere died on his way back from the tournament having fallen asleep at the wheel of his car. The lack of skid marks led to an enquiry and the truth soon emerged, followed in 2006 by a lengthy jail sentence. Perhaps not as wantonly mad as Dokic, but even more deadly.

EDMUNDO

The animal

He calls himself 'O Animal', refers to himself in the third person and encourages his fans to bring tortoises to matches so that they can lob them onto the pitch when he scores. Edmundo is one classy guy by any yardstick, let alone his own.

The nickname actually came from his love of scoring goals, for which he says he has an animal longing, but he has become more famous for his other animalistic monkey business. He offered up endless headlines and a peep into his dark soul in 2000 when he was arrested for force-feeding beer to a chimp called Pedrinho he'd hired for his one-year-old son's birthday party. Fortunately for the police, the case wasn't difficult to prove: Edmundo

Edmundo

had bought a camera and insisted the event was recorded for posterity.

In fact, despite being one of the most gifted footballers of his generation in a country that rules the roost in the beautiful game, what Edmundo gets up to off the pitch is as likely to get him noticed as anything he does on a Saturday afternoon. He is, for instance, currently doing his best to avoid the four-year jail sentence he earned himself for crashing his truck into a row of pedestrians in 1995, killing three people and leading to a manslaughter conviction.

Edmundo hasn't served anything like the full sentence. In fact, he has only served one day; but then Edmundo doesn't much like jail. He proved that in a match in Ecuador when playing for his then club Palmeiras. In a rage because he had missed a penalty, he ran across to the touchline and kicked a television cameraman in the face before holing up in a hotel room when the local bobbies tried enforcing a three-day jail sentence.

The Animal's antics aren't just confined to those who can't hit back though. In Brazil he started a mass brawl at the Palmeiras versus Sao Paulo match when he lamped the tiny midfielder Juninho before going for one of the Sao Paulo directors. After instigating the barney, Edmundo insisted that next time he'd bring his kid nephew because 'it would be fairer' than walloping Juninho, who is 'half a man'.

As if that wasn't all enough, Edmundo earned himself a 120-day ban for slapping referee Sidrack Marinho to go with an earlier 40-day ban for manhandling a referee. He has also earned himself a ban for assaulting a fan in the stadium car park, has been fired by national coach Mario Zagallo for elbowing an opponent off the ball, has been accused of starting a brawl with racist abuse of an opposing player, and has been suspended and fined by his club for repeated public drunkenness. Not that the latter character-trait should have surprised Palmeiras: when he was at Fiorentina in Serie A he negotiated a clause in his contract which allowed him to visit night-clubs at any time of his choosing during the season. That all went wrong when he decided to visit a nightclub in Rio during the carnival and was promptly fired by Fiorentina.

At least Edmundo enjoys the tranquillity that comes with self-knowledge. Holding the record for being sent off seven times in one Brazilian season, he told a bunch of young Vasco Da Gama players in 2003: 'If you listen to what Edmundo says, you might become great players and noble men. If you do what Edmundo does, perhaps not.'

BETHANY HAMILTON

An uplifting madness

Amongst the litany of creeps, weirdos, psychopaths, and dedicated eccentrics that litter these pages, a few stories of unnatural heroism stand out. None are more inspiring than the story of teenage American surfer Bethany Hamilton.

One of the USA's most precocious young sports stars, the pretty blonde 13-year-old already had a sponsorship deal with RipCurl and seemed destined for a professional career when her life changed forever at 7.30 a.m. on Halloween 2003. Resting on her surf board with her arm dangling in the Pacific Ocean in Napali Bay, an area of Kauai, Hawaii, which had never seen a shark attack, a 14ft tiger shark punched through the water beneath Hamilton, hitting her at speed, biting off an 18-inch chunk of her surfboard, and ripping off her left arm just below the shoulder.

'It was kinda like a blur. My arm was hanging in the water and it just came and bit me,' she said. 'It kinda pulled me back and forth, but I just held on to my board and then it let go.' With the help of her best friend Alana Blanchard, Alana's father and brother, and the six other surfers practising nearby, Hamilton was dragged onto the beach where a tourniquet was applied. That's when everything went black, she says. The next thing she knew, she was waking up in hospital minus her left arm.

Her reaction to the tragedy was in many ways guided by her family's deep Christian faith ('I can't change it. That was God's plan for my life and I'm going to go with it') and by a determination to use her fame to good effect. And that's what she's done ever since: in the Thai town of Phuket she slowly walked one trembling eight-year-old boy who had lost his parents and two brothers in the tsunami into the breaking waves after telling him of her own catastrophe. She has raised funds for Hurricane Katrina victims, entertained children with cancer and visited soldiers and Iraqi amputees at three American military hospitals in Germany. She has written a best-selling book, a movie of her life called *Soul Surfer* started shooting in 2005 and she was awarded a slew of honours in the States.

Facing up to the loss of a limb takes immense courage, of course, but Hamilton achieved fame for the way in which she managed to override her own fear and get back in the water *less than three weeks* after she had her arm ripped off. Even though the guilty shark had long since been caught, that took a crazy amount of courage. Yet Hamilton never gave the option of giving up a glance, never worried that she would again be surfing over the top of tiger sharks.

One interviewer famously asked her to talk him through the significance of getting back on a surfboard for the first time on Thanksgiving Day, clearly expecting some tear-jerkingly saccharine explanation. 'Actually, I didn't choose go out on Thanksgiving,' said Hamilton. 'If I was to choose, I'd be out right now but my doctor told me I couldn't go out because on Thursday I got my stitches out, and he said to wait a week. And so, Thanksgiving was just the day.'

Not only has Hamilton confronted her disability, but she has overcome it. She may not fulfil her full potential, but it won't be through lack of effort: within days of the attack she was working out manically, and on 10 January 2004 – just ten weeks after the fateful day – she finished fifth in a national competition. A little over a year later she won her first ever title. It won't be the last for a girl with a glorious sort of madness.

LOU DUROCHER

Nice guys finish last

If Lou 'The Lip' Durocher has one legacy, it's the catch phrase he coined which later went on to be the name of his autobiography: 'nice guys finish last'. The famed baseball slugger and manager once told an interviewer that 'unless a player would kick his grandmother's top [dental] plate out to score a run, he didn't belong in the game'. Among his least admirable qualities was his habit of dropping $100 notes in the lockers of pitchers willing to go for the head, a practice that resulted in several fatalities.

He was a sublime player and manager, one who took part in the famous 1951 game in which the New York Giants' Bobby Thomson hit the 'shot heard round the world' and who competed for the World Series three times and won it once. Yet all of that was overshadowed by a character so noxious that, until his death in 1991, the baseball legends at the Hall of Fame steadfastly refused to induct him on the grounds that they all loathed him.

It's hardly surprising that his peers didn't like him when even Babe Ruth was driven to violence when the two shared a room during their time together at the New York Yankees. In fact, it was the fall-out with Ruth that led to the Yankees trading Durocher to the Cincinnati Reds in 1930, when Ruth proved that Durocher was stealing money and jewellery from his room by leaving marked notes in his wallet. Ruth apparently beat the bejesus out of Durocher, retrieving a long-lost watch in the process. It didn't help that Durocher, a serial gambler, had asked manager Ed Barrow for $1,000 to pay a hotel bill. When

Barrow turned him down, Durocher lost it and roundly abused him. Cue The Lip's departure.

Durocher was a pro at the card table and a devotee of the horse track. He lived life in the fast lane, dating a succession of starlets before marrying beautiful actress Lorraine Day, hanging out with gangsters, and starting feuds. The finest of these was an ongoing hatred with rival batter Casey Stengel, with the two men agreeing to settle their differences *mano-a-mano* in May 1936 beneath the stands at the Brooklyn Dodgers' Ebbets Field. Durocher emerged with a cut lip and Stengel with a bruised eye. Durocher's nickname was also well deserved: he just didn't know when to keep it shut. A tirade against unions while at the Cardinals in 1935 led to the ground being picketed, while in 1940 he picked up the first of many suspensions and fines for 'inciting a riot' at Ebbets Field.

Durocher liked to get in opponents' faces, and in 1942 almost came to grief when, as manager of the LA Dodgers' side playing the Cuban All-Stars in Havana, he behaved so offensively towards his hosts that he sparked a crowd invasion and had to run for his life. He liked close escapes: his next scrape came when he was arrested for slugging a fan being held by a cop. The fan, John Christian, eventually accepted $6,750 to go away, but in many ways the damage had already been done. Durocher's friendship with mobsters like Bugsy Siegel and colourful celebrities like Frank Sinatra hadn't gone unnoticed, and in 1947, shortly after he was condemned by the Catholic Youth Organization for "undermining the moral training of Brooklyn's Roman Catholic youth', he was suspended for the 1947 season by Commissioner Happy Chandler for 'conduct detrimental to baseball' due to his friendship with known gamblers.

The fines continued to come, with the three suspensions and fines in 1952 a high-water mark, but the brash, abrasive, umpire-baiting bench jockey just couldn't care less. Nobody liked him, but after several epic confrontations it was umpires who hated him the most; they even began to penalize his teams wherever possible.

The bible of pro baseball, Karst and Freeman's *Who's Who in Professional Baseball*, spoke for the vast majority of baseball fans and players when it described Durocher. 'Synonymous with controversy, noise, argument, shouting, rhubarbs [fights] and litigation, Durocher has been supreme egotist, brash loudmouth, natural ham, narcissistic monologist, hunch player, strategist. Has been a strutting clothes horse, manicured, pedicured, perfumed, ruthless, sarcastic, bitter, amiable, flirtatious, charming, dapper.' That probably covers about half of it.

ROLLEN STEWART

The rainbow warrior

In the land of the fruitcake, Rainbow-bewigged Rollen Stewart is the fruitiest of them all. Minister, self-appointed scourge of the media, and pest-in-chief for the television networks, Stewart is the classic case of the man who just didn't know when to stop. In the end, only a 120-year jail sentence saved the sporting world from the rainbow warrior.

Rockin' Rollen Stewart first entered the American sporting public's consciousness in 1977 at a Portland Trailblazers basketball game when he managed to station himself courtside in an unmissable position. Not that Stewart was easy to miss: he had a huge rainbow afro wig on his head, a manic smile, a wide-eyed grin, no clothes except for a fake fur loincloth, and a huge placard bearing biblical passages. Oh, and he continually jumped around, trying for all the world to draw attention to himself and spread the Word of the Lord.

Stewart said he 'despised' sport, but over the next two years he would appear at over 200 major live events, quickly becoming expert at stationing himself in the single most visible spot. Occasionally he would be ejected from sporting events, such as the Winter Olympics in Sarajevo,

when the Muslims believed his 'JOHN 3:16' placard was some coded message.

In that annoying way of all weirdos, for a while Stewart became the story – and he liked it that way. Fuelled by vast quantities of marijuana, the reverend nutcase and his new wife Margaret were the scourge of the television companies which, incidentally, he believed were controlled by Satan. Living with Stewart can't have been easy though: at the 1986 World Series at New York's Shea Stadium, Margaret incurred the wrath of the rainbow warrior when she stood in the wrong position. Naturally enough, he tried to throttle her. Equally naturally, she filed for a quickie divorce and ran like the clappers.

Magaret-less, Stewart's barmy behaviour escalated rapidly to the point where the police became seriously concerned. After letting off foul-smelling stink bombs in public offices in Orange County, California, in 1991, he targeted sport again. This time it was golf, with the rainbow man no longer believing that visibility is next to godliness. This time he got himself ejected from the 1991 Masters when he set off a remote controlled air horn, a loud buzzer, and several multi-coloured smoke bombs as Jack Nicklaus was standing over a putt on the 16th green. A similar scenario followed at the world heavyweight fight between George Foreman and Evander Holyfield in 1991, only this time there were so many pyrotechnics in the ring that virtually nobody noticed.

By now, the wiggy one was lurching out of control and was expanding his repertoire. He was arrested for tossing sacks of skunks at performers during the American Music Awards in Los Angeles in 1990 (he said he wanted to show the viewers that 'God thinks this stinks'), and police later found that he'd bought a pistol and had been stalking both president George Bush and presidential candidate Bill Clinton with a view to testing his marksmanship.

The end was in sight though, and when it came it was spectacular. Convinced that Judgement Day was close at hand and wanting to alert the world, in September 1992 Stewart took a maid hostage and barricaded himself in a seventh-floor room at LA's Hyatt Airport Hotel, lighting two fires and taking pot-shots at passing planes for good measure. Cue the arrival of SWAT teams wielding stun grenades which they used quickly and with malice aforethought. Unsurprisingly, the judge didn't take too kindly to the discovery that as well as his multi-coloured afro wig and a pistol, he was cradling an apocalyptic passage from the bible: 'The heavens shall pass away with a great noise, and the elements shall melt with fervent heat'. The result? Three life terms. Harsh but, in the opinion of all right-minded sporting couch-potatoes, fair enough.

Although his flock now consists of seven men who gather for prayers each morning outside the psychiatric services centre at the California State Prison in Sacramento, Stewart remains unrepentant. 'Look at all of the apostles who were persecuted for their faith,' he said from a prison pay phone. 'I did what I thought I had to do. We're talking about eternity here.'

BILLY MARTIN

Slugger extraordinaire

Billy 'The Kid' Martin was a slugger in every sense and the heir apparent to badly behaved baseball legend Lou Durocher. Where his predecessor was a player of quality who could inspire average players to greatness and managed three World Series teams and one winner, four-time manager of the season Martin shared all those managerial characteristics and had two World Series teams, including one winner. Yet that is where the similarities end: Durocher's weakness was his venality and gambling; scrapper Martin's was his total inability to turn the other cheek.

The result was a glittering career punctuated by almighty brawls, which in turn produced a turbulent love-hate relationship with New York Yankees owner George Steinbrenner, who hired and fired Martin five times but

95

who thought enough of him to personally pay for his funeral plot next to Babe Ruth when he died aged 61 on Christmas Day 1989 in a car crash.

The truculence and determination to win at any cost which made him the MVP (Most Valuable Player) in the 1953 World Series and ensured he was such a successful manager, also proved his biggest flaws. His volatility was apparent as early as 1952 when he exchanged insults and punches in the tunnel with Boston's Jimmy Piersall and the next thirty-two years were characterized by a virtually never-ending series of brawls which included fights with two of his own pitchers, a scrap with two travelling team secretaries, and going head-to-head in the dugout on live television with his own team's superstar, Reggie Jackson. As well as beating up a famous national sportswriter, breaking an opposing pitcher's cheekbone (Martin was sued for $1m), scuffling with members of the public, and being fined and suspended for his part in two mass brawls – the footage of 5ft 11in Martin taking on 6ft 11in Gene Conley during fifteen minutes of mayhem in Philly is epic entertainment – Martin took part in two fights which seemed somehow to define his career.

The first happened on his 29th birthday, in May 1957, when a visit to Manhattan's Copacabana Club with Yogi Berra, Mickey Mantle, Whitey Ford, and Hank Bauer to see Sammy Davis Jr. ended in a brawl which sparked a grand jury investigation, $5000 of fines, and his first sacking by Steinbrenner. It was an episode from which his relations with the Yankees never recovered.

The second was a famous 1979 bar-room brawl with a Minnesota marshmallow salesman called Joseph Cooper. Even worse than the Copacabana episode, Marshmallowgate made Martin into a figure of fun. Predictably, that sent him ballistic. The next year, making his return to the city, he had to be physically dragged from the field of play to stop him attacking a section of fans who were pelting him with marshmallows. A sad end to the career of a talented but uncontrollable nutcase.

JEFF TARANGO

Slap-happy

With the possible exception of the ranting John McEnroe, there have been lamentably few tennis nutcases to set the pulses racing, although the Dads From Hell have done their best to hold up their sport's end. One of only four players from this oh-so-civilized sport who does make the cut, though, is American Jeff Tarango. When combined with his obnoxious wife Benedicte, they make a couple capable of exploding through the bad behaviour barrier.

Tarango was famously nutty, not least because he was an obsessive fan of McEnroe's 'assertiveness' – Superbrat famously called a Davis Cup line judge 'a communist pig' and was scratched mid-match during the 1990 Australian Open when he told British umpire Gerry Armstrong to 'just go fuck your mother' – which probably explains some of Tarango's more colourful episodes. Chief among these was one half-hour of berserk behaviour which encapsulates his perpetually deranged state. It occurred during a third-round match at Wimbledon in 1995 when the grumpy Californian – a limited player, his idol Big Mac had more talent in his big toe than Jeff had in his whole body – was on the verge of a rare excursion into the latter rounds of a Grand Slam tournament.

That's when it all went wrong. Playing against Alexander Mronz on centre court, the contest was reaching its tipping point when Tarango banged over an ace. Well, at least he thought he did. Unfortunately, umpire Bruno Rebeuh didn't agree and incorrectly overruled the linesman. Tarango complained, at first legitimately, arguing that the call was too marginal to overrule. When Rebeuh refused to budge, Tarango began to lose the plot. When he was given a code violation warning for wasting time, he really lost it, screaming 'no way' at Rebeuh before informing him that 'you are the most corrupt official in the game, I'm not playing any more' before stomping off the court.

Just in case being defaulted at a Grand Slam tournament wasn't enough to get her husband into real trouble, Tarango's equally insane wife Benedicte added her own physical dimension, striding onto the court and slapping Rebeuh as he tried to make a hasty exit via the tunnel. As Benedicte said in a moment of rare clarity: 'If Jeff had done it, he would have been put out of tennis.'

Although Tarango was fined £30,000 and banned from Wimbledon the next year, he didn't seem to have learned the lesson. In 2000, the hallowed corridors of the All England Club once again rang with the sound of Jeff throwing a wobbly. This time Tarango was booed off court for refusing to shake hands with lowly-ranked Paul Goldstein after going out on a double fault 3–6, 6–2, 5–7, 6–2, 12–10. The American then went on to accuse his young opponent of cheating, impugning the integrity and physical endurance of half the planet as he did so. 'He called the trainer twice on my serve at the end. He runs like a deer, so I don't think he was that hurt,' said Tarango. 'Of course he was faking the injury. Cramping is no reason to get a trainer, maybe for the girls not the guys.'

Despite the charmless Tarango's entertainingly bonkers histrionics, the galleries never warmed to him as they had with Ilie Nastase, Jimmy Connors or even McEnroe. Asked why that may be, his father observed wryly: 'Society will accept you if you are a jerk and win.' An even more appropriate sporting epitaph was the following admission by the nicest guy in tennis, Aussie Pat Rafter: 'Tarango was just so infuriating that there were days when I just wanted to jump over the net and beat the shit out of him.'

EARL COCHELL

Big Mac's role model

If you think of tennis players behaving badly, you inevitably think of John McEnroe and Jeff Tarango, yet they are barely fit to be mentioned in the same breath as tennis's original bad boy, Earl Cochell. Bad and almost certainly mad, the lunatic American remains the only player ever to have been barred for life by the United States Tennis Association.

Generally accepted to have been demented, Cochell was also unfortunate enough to have been obsessively argumentative in an era when it was frowned upon to take issue with officials. Not that this stopped Cochell from becoming involved in a series of heated disputes with umpires.

Yet it is for his 1951 *tour de force* at the US Nationals that he will be forever remembered. A hard-hitting serve and volleyer who could beat anyone on his day, the 29-year-old was a player on the up, and was ranked No.7 in the States going into what would prove to be the last tournament of his career. His fourth-round match with the highly rated Gardner Mulloy was in the balance until a contentious line call sent the highly-strung Cochell over the edge.

As he pleaded with umpire Ellsworth Davenport to overrule the call, the crowd at Forest Hills began to get restless and were soon jeering the player. Never one to take criticism personally, Cochell threw his racquet at a ballboy and yelled at the crowd to shut up.

Predictably, the noise from the cheap seats increased rapidly, at which point Cochell tried to scale the umpire's chair and commandeer the microphone. 'Let me talk to those sons-of-bitches,' he screamed at Davenport. The veteran umpire, though, was having none of it and pushed him back down. With a crowd near mutiny and booing continually, Cochell served out the third set underarm.

As if that wasn't bad enough, Cochell then committed the *faux pas* which saw him suspended indefinitely and summarily dropped from the rankings for what the *Official USTA Yearbook* rather stodgily termed 'unbelievably unfortunate behavior'. During the break between sets, Davenport attempted to defuse a potentially incendiary situation, urging Cochell to calm down. Without even looking up, the No.7 seed said simply: 'Go shit in your hat'. Mulloy won the match without further incident, but Cochell never featured in a match of any consequence again.

His legacy lives on though. Although McEnroe and Tarango are two of his best-known protégés, they are by no means the only ones. In the Eighties, racquet-chucking Fritz Beuhning took madness to Cochellian heights virtually every week. 'He'd swear at you and then he'd turn around and start swearing at your wife, hoping to upset you,' said the Australian Peter McNamara. 'At each change of ends he would chest you, and when he won a trophy he would throw it out his hotel bedroom window the next day. Basically he was mad, but he'd never harm you. He was just a big teddybear.'

The other main 'bumper' was Romania's Irina Spirlea, who chest-bumped Venus Williams in the 1997 US Open, was defaulted and fined a record $20,000 for abusing an umpire in Palermo, Italy. As for racquet-chuckers, there have been an endless succession of those, but amongst the most amusing instances was when dainty drama queen Martina Hingis was playing Steffi Graf at the 1999 French Open and was deducted a point for smashing her racquet, following which she initially refused to play and then staged a glorious exhibition of petulance, serving out the game underarm. Finally, no mention of racquet-chucking would be complete without adding the antics of the crazy Croat Goran Ivanisevic. At the Samsung Open in Brighton in 2000 he smashed all three of his racquets, before realizing he had none left and had to default.

My personal favourite bit of bad behaviour, however, goes to Andre Agassi, for spitting on Australian umpire Wayne McKewan's shoes and trousers in the 1990 US Open, and for getting away with a paltry $500 fine.

MARVIN BARNES

Bad to the bone

Never did a man warrant his nickname more than basketball's Marvin 'Bad News' Barnes, one of the greatest talents squandered in any sport at any time. The 6ft 9in St Louis Spirits player could have been one of the greatest players in NBA history, but instead he'll be remembered for the cocaine, guns, heroin, prostitutes, booze, homelessness, four jail sentences, and nineteen stints in rehab. At one stage, while playing for the Boston Celtics, his cocaine addiction got so bad that he was snorting at courtside during a game, his head hidden under a towel while embarrassed team-mate Nate Archibald bumshuffled away from him.

After a tough childhood on the wrong side of the tracks, with a sister who was a heroin addict and an alcoholic father who was frequently AWOL, Barnes was always struggling against circumstance. Only he didn't struggle too hard. As he says: 'I took pride in being a bad guy. When I was in St Louis (1974–1976), all my friends were pimps, gangsters and drug dealers, and I was kinda drawn to that life.'

'Bad News' earned his nickname at college when he beat team-mate Larry Ketvirtis insensible with an iron tyre lever. He'd already staged armed robberies on grocery stores as a schoolkid, but from college it was all downhill for the incredibly talented but easily-led Barnes. The signs were there at St Louis, when halfway into a rookie season of record-breaking stats, he simply disappeared. A few days later a private detective tracked Barnes and his agent to an illegal pool tournament held in a smoky bar in Dayton, Ohio.

Although Barnes returned and continued his spectacular form, averaging 54 points a game, a pattern had been set.

Barnes was already a slave to cocaine by the time he left the Spirits for the Celtics. Completely wired, he once famously refused to board a TWA flight carrying the Spirits because it was scheduled to leave Louisville at 8 a.m. (eastern time) and arrive in St. Louis at 7.57 a.m. (central time). Barnes just said, over and over, 'I ain't boarding no time machine.'

Over the coming years, Barnes staged a virtuoso

display of life-threatening behaviour as epic as any witnessed in sporting history. He used to travel to Celtics
away games with a pair of hookers stowed on the team
plane, and when he showed up at training he'd stick his
two handguns (a .45 and a .38) in his locker. His body
struggled to hold up as his prodigious drinking, whoring,
and drug-taking took a terrible toll, but Barnes carried
on as though he had a death-wish. 'I was young, I was
wild and I thought I knew everything,' he said. 'I was
doomed. I never thought I was going to live past thirty. I
wanted to die in a shootout. I didn't want a long life. It
wasn't my ambition to live long. You know, live fast and
die young. That was my goal.'

It was one of the few goals he almost achieved. Once
the Celtics had discarded him, he slipped into a life of
crime, serving four prison terms – in Rhode Island, Texas
(where he almost beat a fellow inmate to death in a fight
over drugs) and California – and was sentenced to jail in
Italy for extortion and drugs before the American
embassy whisked him over the border into Yugoslavia in
a cab. Homeless and destitute for much of the time when
he wasn't in jail, a recent god-inspired and drug-free
period of sobriety saw him launch a programme called
'Rebound' to help young kids tempted by drugs and alcohol. Although HBO are thinking about making a film of
his life, Bad News still cuts an unmistakeable figure, turning up for a meeting at the TV company's headquarters

NOTORIOUS

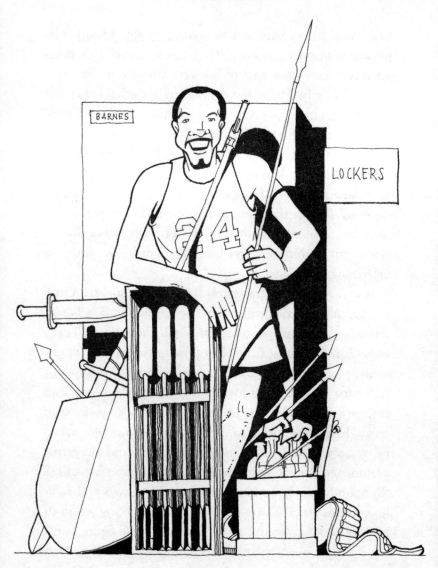

in a chauffeur-driven limousine, wearing dark shades, a diamond ring on each finger and a white, floor-length fur coat.

STUEY 'THE KID' UNGAR

Gin was his tonic

Over the course of thirty years as a professional gambler, Stuey 'The Kid' Ungar lost over $20m betting on sports and horses and made considerably more. And that's even before you factor in what he won and lost with a deck of cards in his hand. Before he died a crack-addled mess of a man in a Las Vegas hotel room without even a tooth-brush to his name, he had become arguably the single greatest gambler of all time. Whether it was as the greatest gin rummy player of all time, the only man ever to win the world championship of poker three times, or the aud-acious punter who once lost $2m on one horse-race, Stuey Ungar lived life to the full.

A bright but troubled kid who hated school but loved cards, it wasn't long before Ungar gravitated towards the latter. Having a photographic memory certainly helped, and when he won a gin rummy tournament aged just 10 while in a holiday resort in the Catskill mountains with

his parents, his life path was firmly mapped out. By the age of 14, he was beating the best players in New York, and when he reached 15 he turned pro and won $10,000 in his first major gin rummy tournament without losing a hand – a record that still stands.

Unfortunately, while Ungar was unbeatable on the card tables – he was so talented that Mafia wiseguys staked him until no one would play him for cash any more – he was not, however, quite such a hit at the horses or on sport, which he would watch obsessively, holed up in his room watching television for days at a time. One week he showed up in Las Vegas with $2m of winnings in his pocket but, banned from most of the casinos, he turned to betting on sport and horses and proceeded to burn through the cash at a staggering rate. By the end of the week he owed $150,000.

In 1980, aged just 24, Ungar entered his first poker world championship and won at a canter. Then he won it again the next year. He staged amazing feats of his prowess in casinos, once betting a fellow punter at Caesars $100,000 that he could forecast each of the next 156 cards to be dealt. He succeeded, and the punter paid up – but the casinos were running scared and Ungar was banned from Caesars and virtually every other casino in Vegas. By then, though, he was making millions in high-stakes games behind closed doors, once taking $5m off porn king Larry Flint during a continuous three-day poker session.

Whilst Ungar was losing heavily on sport and horses, he was also sliding heavily into a dependency upon drugs. Like the best gamblers, Ungar wasn't motivated by possessions but by risk. He would, for example, back himself heavily on the golf course despite not being able to break 100; he even lost $80,000 on the putting green before his first ever round of golf. Ungar didn't even own a watch or bank account and had absolutely no concept of night or day. An absentee father and husband, he had none of the usual trappings of normality. He was, as his biographer Nolan Dalla said, 'a card savant'.

By the time he scraped together $10,000 to enter the 1997 world series of poker he was discounted as a serious punter by the cream of the world's gambling fraternity. He was a shell of a man with a nose so ravaged by coke that it was literally falling off, but Ungar had one last hurrah, hogging the table and cowing the opposition with enormous bets as he swept to victory and collected the $1m cash prize to become the only man to have won three world series of poker. That record, along with winning ten of the thirty major no-limit Hold 'Em tournaments he entered, is one no one else will ever beat.

That, though, was one last bright flicker of the flame before it went out. Two months later he was dead of drugs, found addicted, broke, and alone in a dingy hotel room, the madness finally at an end. He was 43.

ANTHONY WADDLES

Punchbag

Even the most ardent boxing anorak will struggle to recall the name of Anthony Waddles, yet he deserves a mention as one of the bravest of pugilists, a man to rank alongside those heavyweights who took on Mike Tyson in his prime. Either that, or he's a genuinely stupid man. But whichever theory you subscribe to, there's no doubt that Waddles is greedy and quite possibly certifiable.

Most scammers try to work out a way of diddling a little old lady out of her savings or of selling pilfered goods at car-boot sales. Not our Anthony. Short of a few bob, he decided the sensible course of action was to go *mano-a-mano* with the best pound-for-pound fighter in the world in that fighter's home town, Pensacola, Florida, while pretending to be someone else. The person he was pretending to be was the unbeaten Texan junior-middleweight Derwin Richards, and the person he stepped into the ring with was Roy Jones Jr, the most deadly fighter since Roberto Duran.

Fortunately, the deception was quickly uncovered. Unfortunately, not before Waddles had taken a mother and father of a beating. For a start, Richards was a cunning, experienced, and durable fighter who would

have given Jones a decent fight, while Waddles was a hopeless rookie who had failed to come close to winning any of his three professional fights. Despite the 19-year-old second-hand car salesman from Oklahoma holding onto Jones like a drowning man, the hometown fighter battered the stand-in senseless, winning the fight in two minutes and two seconds of the first round.

When puzzled boxing writers rang Richards to find out why he'd folded so quickly, an equally puzzled fighter denied having been in Pensacola. 'Say what? I was definitely not there,' said Richards. 'I would like to fight Roy Jones, but that wasn't me fighting.' The Texan, it turns out, is a guard at a maximum-security prison and was on duty at the time, with his every move captured on closed-circuit television.

Although Waddles initially managed to escape censure (although being battered by Jones probably counts as punishment enough in most people's book), police quickly arrested Oklahoma promoter Elvis Belt and Memphis match-fixer Gerome Peete on charges of grand theft by fraud, with both of them facing up to five years in prison if found guilty of fraudulently collecting the $2,000 purse. They even defrauded Waddles if he is to be believed.

'Elvis Belt contacted me and said he may have a fight for me,' Waddles said. 'He said I could make some good money, something like $2,000 for this fight, but I wasn't supposed to do nothing expect fight. I only got paid $700 though. Man, he stiffed me, too – I knew it would happen.'

Unfortunately for Waddles, it seems that he is as good at lying as he is at fighting. Tommy Griggs, an accountant employed by the Pensacola promoters, testified that he witnessed the impostor sign a settlement sheet and endorse a $1,960 cheque for his purse with Richards' signature. All of which put Waddles back in the frame in the police enquiry.

So Waddles, who hails from Norman, Oklahoma, had driven for ten hours across several states for the chance to get his face pummelled in a no-win contest against the hardest-punching man on the planet, for which he could get sent to prison for five years and have a criminal record for the rest of his life. And all for $700. Now that's madness.

GEOFFREY HUISH

Showed real balls

Fanatical rugby fan Geoff Huish was so convinced that his beloved Wales would lose to England during the 2005 Six Nations tournament that he told fellow drinkers in

Senghenydd, near Caerphilly that 'I will cut my bollocks off if Wales win'. It was, thought his friends, just drunken banter. They were wrong.

It was only when Welsh centre Gavin Henson banged over a huge penalty at the death to give Wales an unlikely 11–9 win, their first against the English in Cardiff for twelve years, that things took a turn for the worse. While packed onlookers in the Leigh Social Club went crazy, 26-year-old Huish walked the 200 yards to his home, took a craft knife and made good on his promise.

'He said he'd cut his balls off if Wales won and he did,' said roofer Paul Shapcott, who was in the club, 'so fair play to him. He came back later wearing a kilt with his testicles in a bag. He lifted the kilt up to show everyone what he had done and said "I've done it – here's my balls". There was blood everywhere, it was terrible. That's when he collapsed.'

Another villager said: 'We're all in a state of shock, no one can believe what happened. He must have been in terrific pain. It was amazing he could walk the 200 yards from his house back to the club. Apparently he's been on medication and shouldn't have been drinking. His family are very upset.'

Huish, who was clearly a troubled young man, handed his balls to bar-staff, who called 999 and then put the bachelor's testicles in a pint glass filled with ice in an unsuccessful attempt to save them. The local medical authorities refused to comment, other than to say that Huish was resting at a mental health unit in Gwent.

MARIO 'MACHITO' GOMEZ

The unwanted party-crasher

South America, the continent that spawned Edmundo and Maradona, is the land of big characters and the sort of life-is-cheap attitude that led to Colombia defender Andres Escobar being gunned down in broad daylight in a bar for the unpardonable offence of letting in a crucial goal in the 1994 World Cup. It is also the continent that spawned Peruvian nutcase Mario 'Machito' Gomez.

A well-known defender with Universitario, Peru's most successful football club, Machito was arrested in December 2002 after gang member Gloria Pilar Prieto died with a bullet to the head and football rival Jorge Farfan Jimenez was shot in the mouth following a disturbance at a party held at a sports club in Callao, near Lima. Machito's cousin, Raul Urbina Bonifaz, whose former girlfriend Edith Chillitupa Concha was left in a coma after the attack, was also arrested. The 21-year-old footballer's father Augusto went on a local TV station and immediately claimed his boy was innocent, but police discovered three bullet shells at the scene of the incident – two from a revolver, and another one from a pistol – with subsequent ballistics tests proving Machito's involvement.

However, the course of true justice doesn't always run smoothly, and in June 2003 Machito was released from prison by the authorities through lack of evidence. Apparently they had trouble finding anyone willing to testify against the defender. He is now back playing with Universitario.

The same doesn't go for another dodgy South American, crazy-haired Colombian goalkeeper Rene Higuita, he of the Wembley 'Scorpion' kick. A friend of Colombia's most notorious drug baron, Higuita has often been viewed with suspicion by the authorities, especially after he tested positive for cocaine in 1993. So when El Loco acted as a go-between in a notorious kidnapping, he ended up doing six months in the Big House. His novel defence – 'I'm a footballer, I didn't know anything about kidnapping laws' – failed to cut much ice with the court.

Higuita is currently launching a comeback, and was last seen having extensive plastic surgery on an Ecuadorian TV Extreme Makeover show. He now looks like a member of Kool And The Gang.

DAI THOMAS

A real hooligan

Being a professional footballer might be every little boy's dream, but it was all too dull for portly Cardiff City striker Dai Thomas. But being a self-starting sort of fella, he was able to liven up his life by joining Cardiff hooligan group the Soul Crew and going on the rampage at Euro 2000.

A former Wales under-21 international, Thomas had the bad luck to be caught on film by a *Panorama* undercover documentary crew investigating the huge levels of right-wing football-related violence at the tournament. When footage of the striker trashing a Brussels bar was shown on British screens, Thomas was immediately sacked by the Welsh club.

However, his career as a hooligan had only just started. In January 2002, while still playing as a semi-professional, Thomas was arrested and jailed for public order offences following the riots at Cardiff's FA Cup third-round clash with Premiership bad boys Leeds United at Ninian Park, which almost had to be abandoned after sustained crowd violence. The 26-year-old was described as one of the ringleaders of the trouble, and magistrates heard how he was recorded by a CCTV camera throwing an advertising hoarding at rival fans. Thomas had little choice but to plead guilty to 'behaviour causing fear and provocation'.

If that was embarrassing for Cardiff City, it was as nothing compared to the concern expressed at Bundesliga club Fortuna Dusseldorf when the activities of former starlet Nizar Trabelsi came to light. The Tunisian international had been signed by Fortuna in 1989 and seemed like a great buy. Strongly integrated and a good player, all went swimmingly until Trabelsi developed a nasty little coke habit and was dropped by the club. He soon descended into petty theft and was sent to jail.

While inside he adopted some radical views and soon became a member of Takfir wal-Hijra, the extreme Islamic group blamed for the assassination of Dutch filmmaker Theo Van Gogh. Following a lengthy trip to Afghanistan, where he says he received orders directly from Osama Bin Laden, in 2003 Trabelsi was convicted of a plot to drive a car bomb into a NATO airbase in Belgium and was sentenced to ten years in prison.

On the subject of Bin Laden, at Highbury opposing fans still joke that Osama Bin Laden is 'hiding in Kabul and supports the Arsenal', a mocking reference to America's Most Wanted's sporting allegiance when he lived in London.

RICHARD VIRENQUE

'I'll try anything'

The Festina Scandal at the 1998 Tour de France marked cycling's low point, the day its dirty little secret was dragged out into the open for the world to see. Cycling was infested with drugs, and on 18 July when Willy Voet, the *soigneur* (literally 'helper') for the highly ranked Festina team, was caught crossing the border between Belgium and France driving a car stacked with vials – 250 doses of the blood-boosting drug EPO (erythropoietin), 100 doses of anabolic steroids and various other illicit substances – le merde hit le fan.

At the centre of the maelstrom of controversy was Richard Virenque, the lead rider for the French team and the star turn of Gallic cycling. The previous year's King of the Mountains and the only Frenchman with a realistic chance of winning Le Tour, the mad lengths to which Virenque was willing to go to win unfolded as soon as Voet was in custody. Voet, abandoned by the sport to which he had devoted thirty poorly-paid years, published a small but incendiary little tome called *Breaking the Chain*, which detailed Virenque's manic quest for any-thing which would give him an edge. And Voet would

Richard Virenque

know: Virenque denied everything, but the rider and Belgian soigneur had been 'like father and son'.

Not only did dad detail what his errant son took to make him cycle faster and further, but he also detailed what Virenque took for recreational purposes. 'Belgian pot' was a ballistic compound of cocaine, caffeine, heroin, amphetamines and cortisone which Virenque and the Festina riders used on nights out, and the revelation marked a turning point from which the sport may never recover, and from which the rider will certainly not come back.

Virenque was not only willing to stick virtually any substance into his body, but he pro-actively supervised the team's doping regime. 'Virenque clearly knew what he was doing,' wrote Voet. 'He was the leader, the chief, and spokesman. Nothing could be decided without consulting him. He was the person who pushed the use of banned substances the most.' The team would pay for the riders' drugs, with the not-insubstantial outlay later being recouped from their prize money, so Virenque knew exactly what he'd been taking and when.

Virenque was the team's heaviest doper, said Voet, one who had told the soigneur when he joined Festina in 1993: 'I will try anything'. He wasn't picky and large chunks of *Breaking the Chain* detail how Voet had to be constantly alert to stop Virenque trying random 'new' rogue substances offered by one of the other soigneurs on the Tour. There was, after all, a high chance that they would react badly to the cocktail of EPO, blood thinners, steroids, steroid-masking agents, amphetamines, testosterone and human growth hormone Virenque routinely used.

From the condoms of clean urine that Virenque kept up his bum to pass dope tests, through to his ingestion of pot Belge, he was an animal for drugs, a cheat as shameless as any that has ever ridden on the Tour, but one who maintained a pathological aversion to admitting that he had an edge over his fellow competitors. Tommy Simpson, who died on Mont Ventoux in the 1967 Tour when extreme heat combined with the amphetamines and brandy in his system to produce a toxic mix, once said: 'If it takes ten (pills) to kill you, I'll take nine'. Those words should have been Virenque's motto. Instead, utterly deluded until the moment he broke down in a Lyon courtroom and confessed his guilt, he called his autobiography *Ma Verite* (My Truth).

CHICAGO WHITE STOCKINGS'
MURDEROUS TRIO

Three of the worst

Although being a criminal or being jailed doesn't make sportsmen mad or eccentric *per se*, the concentration of felons at the Chicago White Stockings at the back end of the nineteenth century is so staggering that it is the one exception in these pages.

The most notable of the deadly trio in the 1880s was Hall of Famer John Clarkson, who won the 1885 MVP Award thanks to winning fifty-three games. Known as quiet, thoughtful, and courteous, the legendary pitcher ascended to the status of Cooperstown deity in 1963, yet it was despite the fact that he'd slashed his wife to death with a razor after retiring (not that you'd know it if you looked at the Hall of Fame's official website). Yet that made him look almost ordinary compared to his two compadres, John Glenn and Terry Larkin.

Although Clarkson got on well with his team-mate Glenn, the younger man bore little resemblance to his staid mentor. Glenn was always wild, so wild in fact that he ended up in prison when a robbery went wrong in 1878. After spending about a year in prison in Rochester, New York, he headed for the small town of Glen Falls on the day he was released. Once there, he hid behind an outhouse and jumped on a passing 12-year-old girl before raping her. When her cries alerted a rampaging mob and Glenn had to take to his heels, a passing policeman, who had been trying to protect Glenn by loosing off a warning shot, 'accidentally' shot him stone dead.

It takes some doing, but the third of the trio, Terry Larkin, was the maddest of the lot. Depressed after he retired in 1880, he slit his own throat and shot his wife. Both survived, however, but Larkin was clearly mentally disturbed and was forcibly moved to an asylum. Once there he went even further downhill and dived headfirst off his bed into a cast-iron radiator. His ever-faithful wife nursed him back to health and, as a token of his gratitude, he spared her but killed her father before cutting his own throat with a razor. This time he made no mistake.

Mind you, at least Larkin's wife wasn't married to Boston Braves catcher Marty Bergen or the Cincinnati Red Stockings pitcher Charles 'Pacer' Smith. In 1899 team-mates said Bergen had been 'overcome by melancholy and had been the subject of much comment among his friends, who were worried by the signs of insanity'. They proved to be right: just after he sustained a career-ending hip injury he killed his wife and two young children with an axe before cutting his own throat with a razor. Smith, meanwhile, shot and killed his five-year-old daughter and teenage sister-in-law and also tried to shoot his wife, and was hanged on 29 November, 1895, making him the only major-leaguer ever executed (bizarrely, former catcher Frank Harris was scheduled to be executed on the same day for murder, but he was reprieved).

ALEX HIGGINS

The people's nutcase

He may have been the ultimate showman, the man who popularised snooker in the early Seventies, but Alex 'Hurricane' Higgins' legacy is as a copper-bottomed madman. Since the day the 16-year-old prodigy failed at his quest to become a jockey and turned to snooker, he was scrapping with colleagues, fighting with officialdom, battling cancer and alcoholism. So stoically mad has the behaviour of the two-time world champion and self-styled 'people's champion' been over the past forty years that it's difficult to know where to start.

Higgins will certainly be remembered by his colleagues. At the 1990 World Team Cup, he initiated snooker's most bitter feud when he got into a row with fellow Northern Ireland team member Dennis Taylor over the order of play and whether the highest break prize should be split. As the two men quarrelled in public, Higgins, a 'visibly

inebriated' Protestant from Belfast's notorious Shankhill Road area, threatened retribution on Taylor, a Catholic from Coalisland. 'I come from the Shankill. The next time you're in Northern Ireland I'll have you shot,' Higgins was alleged to have said. Not one to make matters worse, Higgins continued: 'Dennis Taylor is not a snooker person. He is a money person. He's not fit to wear this badge, the red hand of Ulster.'

The source of Higgins' wrath was the fact that Northern Ireland had just been beaten by a Canadian team featuring Cliff Thorburn, another player who had a long-standing feud with the Hurricane. A former hustler who'd seen the seedy side of life, Thorburn wasn't going to be cowed by Higgins. Their first clash came in 1973 when Higgins borrowed £50 from Thorburn during a card game, handing over his wedding ring as collateral. Higgins' wife Cara wasn't impressed and later that night the two of them came looking for the ring. 'Alex pretended to fall down in a faint. I attempted to pick him up, then turned my back on him and he went for me with a bottle,' said Thorburn. 'I grabbed him, threw the bottle down, got him round the neck and just pounded his head until my fist was sore.'

The next time the two men met on the snooker table, Higgins beat Thorburn and, as the loser was leaving, the Irishman called him 'a Canadian cunt'. Thorburn smashed him in the face, and was about to drag him outside to administer more admonishment when he was pulled off a crumpled Higgins.

Violence was as integral to Higgins' life as the alcohol which fuelled his rage. He will be remembered forever for assaulting referee Len Ganley, but his most insane episode occurred at a tournament in Preston in 1986 when a request to take a drugs test sent a pissed Higgins mental. After assaulting the doctor, he punched one tournament official and then head-butted another.

Only the arrival of a security guard stopped Higgins from dispatching the second official, who he was by now throttling in earnest. Covered in blood, he ran off to his dressing room, where he punched a hole in the door and three in the wall. As a posse of security guards rushed to confront him, Higgins ran down the corridor, grabbing a pile of dinner plates left behind by caterers and skimming them like Frisbees at his pursuers. Eventually over-powered, Higgins stubbed out the fag hanging from his mouth on a guard's hand. He was later fined £12,000 and banned from five tournaments.

His relations with women were similarly troubled. Once, after a blazing three-hour row with then partner, psychologist Siobhan Kidd, Higgins fell out of the window of her first-floor flat, smashing his ankle and cutting his head. He was so drunk that she'd locked the door to stop him going to the pub, and he had forgotten they were not on the ground floor. When he got out of hospital and beat her with a hair dryer, she called it quits. In 1997, when he broke a court order forbidding him from 'molesting, assaulting, or communicating' with his latest girlfriend, former Manchester hooker Holly Haise, and drunkenly barged into her flat, she stabbed him three times.

As *Hurricane*, a one-man show about Higgins' life, showed, drink was the key to his problems – he once drank a tumbler of Giorgio Armani aftershave to win a bet with long-time drinking buddy Ollie Reed – but in truth it only exacerbated his deeply flawed and deeply unpleasant character.

MIKE TYSON

Saddest man on the planet

No list of nutters would be complete without the self-styled Baddest Man on the Planet. Rapist, road rage specialist, press conference brawler, wife-beater, ear-chewer, Muslim convert, jailbird, and all-round pathetic man-child, 'Iron' Mike Tyson was one of the most powerful, intimidating heavyweight champions of all time, but will be remembered as much for what he was outside the ring as for what he did in it. From a man with the world at his feet, Tyson became a deranged pariah, a friendless freak show who burned his way through $400m in two decades and who enters his forties with debts of $35m.

The story of how he was mentally scarred as a young man is well known and probably overblown. Legend has it that the young Tyson, growing up in a dysfunctional home in a New York ghetto, was fairly well adjusted until a local hood killed his beloved pigeons and unleashed the monster within. First convicted for purse snatching in 1978 as a 12-year-old, he was sent to reform school, which was where he came under the wing of Catskills guru Cus D'Amato the next year. In the accepted version, the veteran trainer provided Tyson with a surrogate father and kept him on the straight and narrow. In reality, even before D'Amato's death in 1984, when Tyson was 18, the future heavyweight champion of the world was a persistent offender.

Tyson's all-action style produced the most compelling boxing viewing since Muhammad Ali hung up his gloves, and when in November 1986 he knocked-out Trevor Berbick in the second round to become the youngest heavyweight world champion in boxing history at 20 years and 144 days, Tyson had money and fame. He also had an increasingly bad temper and a mistaken belief that he was bulletproof.

Women were a major flaw. The first of many out-of-court settlements came in 1987 when a parking attendant

intervened to save a woman Tyson was trying to kiss and the boxer battered him senseless. The next year he married actress Robin Givens, who proceeded to spend every bit of money she could get her hands on, even suing for access to funds to buy a $3m New Jersey mansion. Amid accusations of wife-beating and irrational behaviour, Givens labelled Tyson 'manic-depressive' on live television, with the boxer responding by trying to commit suicide by driving his car into a tree outside D'Amato's home, succeeding only in knocking himself unconscious.

Tyson's marriage to Givens and subsequent divorce seemed to unleash a rage within the heavyweight, and he quickly began to unravel. A comic brawl with former opponent Mitch 'Blood' Green in a Harlem department store saw him break his right hand, but being arrested one day for slapping a parking attendant outside an LA nightclub and then being fined $200 and sentenced to community service for speeding the next, seemed to indicate that he was sliding out of control.

In 1990, the unthinkable happened when 42–1 shot James 'Buster' Douglas knocked out Tyson. From there it was downhill all the way, both in and out of the ring. Within weeks he was successfully sued by Givens' former aide for sexual assault and harassment and then found guilty by a New York court of committing battery against Sandra Miller. The next year he admitted paternity of an eight-month-old daughter, and was then found guilty in

Indianapolis of raping 18-year-old beauty queen Desiree Washington. He was sentenced to six years, but only served three.

A tattooed convert to Islam in prison and now embroiled in a destructive relationship with promoter Don King, Tyson's main appeal now was his notoriety. But after beating a couple of lowly-ranked fighters – including Briton Frank Bruno, from whom he took the WBC title – Tyson was beaten for the second time in a year by Evander Holyfield. If his career as a serious fighter was almost over by then, Tyson killed it stone dead in 1997 when, in the second and final meeting with Holyfield, he bit most of the champion's left ear off. The sight of the bloody rump of Holyfield's ear lying on the canvas is still one of the most sickening images ever conjured up by sport.

With his falsetto voice and bull-necked swagger, there had always been a freak-show element to Tyson's appeal, but from there his life quickly spiralled downwards. Fined £3m and suspended from boxing for the ear-biting episode, his behaviour – and that of his huge band of homies – became increasingly erratic. In 1998 he punched and kicked two motorists after a traffic accident, earning himself three months in prison, a month of which he spent in solitary after trashing his cell. Knocked out in the eighth round in 2002 after being comprehensively outclassed by Lennox Lewis– whose leg he bit during a hugely entertaining mass brawl at the pre-fight press conference – Tyson, by now sporting a ludicrous Polynesian tattoo across his face, finally retired when beaten in 2005 by little-fancied Irishman Kevin McBride. A sad end to a stellar career – although there may yet be worse to come from the most self-destructive fighter of them all.

DIEGO MARADONA

The nose of God

Diego Armando Maradona is to football what Mike Tyson is to boxing, a poor little boy from the ghetto who found it difficult to handle his fame and who eventually let his base instincts rule his life. But where violence and testosterone-driven machismo were Tyson's creed, the greatest footballer the world has ever known had equally basic preoccupations: sex and drugs and not in that order.

Maradona was first introduced to cocaine when he was at Napoli in 1983 and was, by his own admission, immediately hooked. For the next twenty years the drug was to define the little Argentine's existence, consuming him bit by bit and then, when there was no more talent or physical prowess to destroy, spitting out a bloated 20-stone caricature.

Despite already being three years down the road to addiction and despair by 1986, it was a sporting year marked by Maradona's brilliance. Making up for the disappointment of the 1982 World Cup, when he was sent off against Brazil as Argentina bombed, he scored five goals in that year's tournament as he almost single-handedly won the trophy for a mediocre Argentina. But it is for the two goals that the No. 10 scored against the hated English 'pirates' – one the famous 'Hand of God', the other, one of the most dazzling dribbled goals ever seen – that he will be forever remembered.

Yet by then Maradona was already in the grip of an addiction that would drive him into a coma and the nut-house. He had morphed from a quiet young man to a larger-than-life character while in Spain with Barcelona, who eventually sold him to Napoli because of his excessive socializing and increasingly risqué choice of nightlife (he once took the whole Seville squad to a Spanish brothel). When he reached Italy, however, his coke-fuelled mania pushed him to another level. From wounding two journalists with an air rifle and siring illegitimate sons to staging coked-up parties attended by the cream of Naples' mafia families, Maradona's life in Italy became one long mad rush towards oblivion.

The Argentine's life changed forever in 1991 when he tested positive for cocaine. Until then the club had ensured he wasn't tested (with good reason: they won the double in his first season and sold 70,000 season tickets for the first time ever), but with his powers fading and his behaviour plummeting, getting his enormous salary off the wage bill was too tempting. Banned for fifteen months, he deteriorated quickly.

To pep himself up he married his long-time sweetheart Claudia. In his trademark ostentatious style, he spent £1m on a Buenos Aires wedding at which an eighty-piece orchestra in tango suits serenaded 1,200 guests, 300 of whom had been flown over from Rome on a chartered Boeing 747. With Claudia wearing a £25,000 dress, the happy couple drove into the ballroom in a Rolls-Royce which had once belonged to Joseph Goebbels. Large amounts of prostitutes and cocaine were provided for guests, naturally.

With his cocaine addiction all-encompassing, each of his five comebacks were abject failures, but the first was the most spectacular fall from grace. Maradona had lost a quarter of his bodyweight in a month so that he could compete at the 1994 World Cup, but the day after scoring in the opening fixture and staging an eye-bulging celebration, he tested positive.

Since then, it seemed only a matter of time until he killed himself. In 1996 he caused uproar when he booked twenty-five hookers to come to his room for drugs, booze, and sex at London's plush Dorchester Hotel (there were so many there that they ended up fighting in the corridors). His Millennium bender was so epic that he almost died of an overdose and was rushed to Cuba (of course!) where he spent nearly four years in rehab. Not that it helped: in 2004 he spent three months in a psychiatric unit in Havana, where he was filmed at a party taking coke and having sex with his 19-year-old girlfriend in front of the other guests. He was dressed as Osama Bin Laden at the time, armed with a toy machine-gun.

Yet there may be hope for Maradona. After spending twelve days in hospital with heart and lung problems that almost killed him (it didn't help when he slept naked in a room with the air conditioning turned up full despite having pneumonia), he has had his stomach stapled and got down to 13 stone. He is even well enough to celebrate when his beloved Boca Juniors score (by diving fully clothed into his pool) and fit enough to take up a new sport, golf (although he only plays at night using luminous balls).

Now the host of an incredibly popular television show, at least Maradona has kept his ego in check. First he admonished Pope John-Paul II for showing him a 'total lack of respect' when they met in Rome and the pontiff gave him the same rosary as everybody else rather than a special one. 'I've been to the Vatican and seen the gold ceilings. And then I hear the Pope saying that the Church was concerned about poor kids. So? Sell the ceilings, mate! You've got nothing going for you. You were only a goalkeeper.' Mind you, ending up with a God-complex after ingesting that much cocaine is no surprise: 'If Jesus stumbled, then why shouldn't I as well?' he said, before adding: 'Diego Maradona will only ascend to Heaven when all four Beatles are waiting to meet him'.

LATRELL SPREWELL

A losing spree

None of basketball star Latrell Sprewell's Golden State Warriors team-mates were in any doubt that he was a nasty piece of work. He had already fought in training with team-mate Byron Houston and become involved in a confrontation with another Warrior, Jerome Kersey in 1995. Not content with trading blows with Kersey, he went outside and returned with a piece of two by four. Then he threatened to return with a gun.

As if that wasn't proof enough of his ill intent, he provided yet more the year before when his four-year-old daughter was attacked by one of his family's four pet pitbulls and had her ear completely severed. Sprewell said that neither he nor the child were traumatised. 'Stuff happens,' he barked at reporters.

The high-water mark of Sprewell's madness was yet to

arrive though. During a practice session in 1997, head coach PJ Carlesimo bawled Sprewell out for not trying hard enough, an everyday occurrence across the sporting world. Sprewell's reaction, however, was completely out of the ordinary: rushing across the court, he grabbed Carlesimo around the throat and started throttling him. Not content with almost killing his boss, Sprewell returned twenty minutes later to finish the job. Unable to finish his spot of strangulation, the player walloped his coach in the face instead.

Suspended for sixty-eight games and fined $6m for the attack, Sprewell also lost his Converse shoe deal. Not that Sprewell, the son of a drugs dealer, ever saw the error of his ways. 'I mean, PJ, he could breathe,' Sprewell said three days later when he finally broke his silence. 'It's not like he was losing air or anything like that. I mean, it wasn't a choke. I wasn't trying to kill PJ.'

With his sense of injustice mounting and his delusional tendencies kicking in, Sprewell insisted he wasn't choking the coach, but was merely 'resting his hands' on Carlesimo's throat; that he didn't come back to hit his coach, but may have 'inadvertently' hit him in the face. None of which squared with the pictures of the coach's red-raw neck which appeared in *Sports Illustrated*: you could still see Sprewell's handprints.

Just to emphasize his nutty credentials, the Warriors guard then sued his agent for failing to negotiate a salary protection clause in his contract. When that didn't work he went after the NBA, suing them for $30m and claiming that he was fired from his three-year $24m contract because three NBA security employees shredded evidence that would have exonerated him. He was, he said, the victim of racial discrimination. He also alleged a wide-ranging conspiracy in which the FBI were the prime movers.

That didn't work, and neither did his defence in his other court case at that time; Sprewell eventually pleading no contest to a reckless driving charge that resulted from him driving into another car at 90mph when he drove the wrong way up an exit to the freeway. He got three months of home detention for that one.

PAUL GASCOIGNE

Dr Gascoigne and Mr Gazza

It's impossible to know where to start with over-emotional man-child Paul Gascoigne. The iconic footballing figure of his generation, he was in almost every way as remarkable as the equally nutty Diego Maradona. Like El Diego, he connected on some level with the public, and never more so than during the 1990 World Cup semi-final against West Germany in Italy when his televised tears at receiving a yellow card (which would have kept him out of the final had England got there) had grannies the length and breadth of the nation reaching for their Kleenex.

A sublimely gifted midfielder, Gascoigne – or Gazza as he quickly became known in the tabloids – was capable of epic highs and horrible lows on the football pitch. His glorious goal for England against Scotland at Wembley at Euro '96 falls into the former category, while the vicious lunge at Nottingham Forest's Gary Charles in the 1991 FA Cup final definitely falls into the latter, not least because it left him with damaged knee ligaments that kept him out of the game for a year.

If Gascoigne was a split personality on the pitch, off it the juvenile joker had more sides than the Champions League. Over the course of a playing career that started in the late Eighties and finished when he was sacked as Kettering player-manager in December 2005 for turning up to training drunk after just 39 days in charge, the full panoply of bad behaviour was played out for the red-tops' delectation. As the *Guardian*'s Simon Hattenstone noted, there were 'the nine nervous ticks, the Tourettesian out-bursts, the bulimia, the phobias, the depression, the pranks, the car crashes, the alcoholism, the benders, the hypochondria, the blackouts, the cocaine, the domestic violence, the non-domestic violence, the 27 operations, the suicidal thoughts. And that's before we even start with the football.'

Gascoigne must have been hell to live with. In his younger days, his hyper-activity was dismissed as youthful exuberance, but it was exhausting. England team-mates begged not to be roomed with him on tour because he couldn't bear to be alone, and would wake room-mates at all times of the night for a chat. The penalty for falling asleep was severe: he once relieved himself over a sleeping Richard Gough while at Rangers. He was also an inveterate prankster who once enlivened the sectarian tinderbox that is the Old Firm derby by mimicking a protestant apprentice boy playing a flute in a cameo plucked straight out of Ulster's incendiary marching season. On another occasion, he put shit sandwiches in the fridge before a drinking session, waiting to see which unwitting soul would eat them. That unlucky drinking companion would probably have been Jimmy 'Five Bellies', Gascoigne's childhood friend from Newcastle and his constant companion. It says much for Gazza's profile that JFB is better known than many Premiership footballers.

Although neither Gascoigne nor his long-suffering and oft-beaten wife Sheryl would have known it, Gascoigne's manic energy, short attention span and childish, inappropriate behaviour all pointed towards a condition known as Attention Deficit Disorder, while his overwhelming anxiety was caused by an Obsessive Compulsive Disorder which could only be relieved by repetitive behaviour, whether that be obsessive tidying, over-exercising, or going on two-day benders with friends like the Gallagher brothers from Oasis or DJ Chris Evans. As all good things come in threes, psychiatrists also informed him that his trademark twitches, grimaces and outbursts are classic symptoms of Tourette's Syndrome.

Gazza realized that he wasn't enjoying being Gazza any more when he stood on a train platform contemplating suicide in 1998. Desperate to change his fortunes, he eventually resorted to changing his name from Paul Gascoigne to G8, and refusing to answer to the name Gazza. Being at the centre of Gazza-mania, it seems, was enough to drive anyone bonkers.

DUNCAN FERGUSON

Duncan Disorderly

His legions of fans on the terraces know him as 'Duncan Disorderly' or 'Drunken Duncan', but legendary Scottish hardman Duncan Ferguson is no laughing matter.

Certainly that's what a Fife sheriff thought in 1994 when he ensured that Ferguson became the first – and so far only – player ever to have been jailed for an on-field assault. Then with Rangers, Big Dunc was in a trademark frenzy when he lost the plot completely and laid the heid on Raith Rovers defender John McStay in front of a packed Stark's Park. Had it been anyone else, he may have got away with it, but Ferguson had 'previous' – and plenty of it – and ended up serving a three-month prison sentence in Glasgow's notorious Barlinnie Jail.

As a young man, rumours circulated of Ferguson entering pubs and offering to fight anyone man enough to take him on. His subsequent dealings with the boys in blue certainly suggest that an appetite for destruction is an integral part of the Ferguson make-up. At various stages before he head-butted McStay, he was arrested for head-butting a policeman after a bender, attacking a man on crutches in a taxi queue, another assault on another unfortunate in a taxi queue (what is it about taxi queues?), plus giving an unlucky Anstruther fisherman a thorough working over after a night on the sauce. When with Rangers, legend has it that he used to light his cigars with a £50 note in order to bait mere mortals.

Although he took up pigeon fancying and moved south of the border after his release from jail, trouble seems to have followed Ferguson wherever he's gone. He missed Everton's pre-season tour to the USA when he was barred as an 'undesirable alien', and he sparked a sixteen-man brawl at Middlesbrough with a criminally late challenge on goalkeeper Mark Schwarzer. In September 2005, Big Dunc was cited by UEFA for allegedly elbowing Dinamo

Bucharest defender Gabriel Tamas in the head in the dying minutes of Everton's UEFA Cup tie in Romania, although he was later to escape a ban.

Bizarrely, though, at least two people were unaware of Dunc's fearsome reputation. The first tried burgling his Formby mansion and was hospitalised for his trouble. The second would-be burglar really pissed Dunc off – as well as a four-year sentence, he also needed two days of emergency dental surgery.

But Ferguson remains a cult hero, one who has another unlikely claim – that he has inspired a piece of classical music. His assault on McStay has been immortalized in a piece by Finnish composer and Everton fanatic, Osmo Tapio Raihala. He has dubbed his new creation Barlinnie Nine, subtitling it 'an ode to underachievement' and premiering it in front of 2,000 people in Helsinki.

'I got the idea for it when he got sent to jail and then became something of a cult figure for Everton,' said Raihala. 'It takes into account the contradictions in him. He has an aggressive side but there is a lyrical undertone to him, as the fact that he keeps pigeons shows.'

TITANIC THOMPSON

The hustler

It says much for Titanic Thompson (real name Alvin Clarence Thomas) that he was the man on whom *Damon* Runyan based his character Sky Masterton, the charismatic gambler in *Guys and Dolls*, yet it's also somehow fitting because Thompson was such an outrageous character that there has been a real danger of the legend fusing with reality. No one still knows, for instance, whether he really earned his nickname by escaping from the Titanic disguised as a woman. Yet of one thing there is absolutely no doubt: Ti (as his friends called him) was the most celebrated hustler of all time.

The roaring Twenties were a time when hustlers lived in folk legend, revered by the masses. Some made such a name for themselves that they are still known today – tennis player Bobby Riggs for his baiting of Billie Jean King, pool player Minnesota Fats for his immortalisation by Runyan – while several of the biggest, men like poker legend Puggy Pearson, backgammon guru Tim Holland, and golf and poker expert Johnny Moss have faded from memory. All of them, though, were pipsqueaks next to Thompson.

Thompson's name was already whispered with awe in

poker halls, pool halls, bars, and golf clubs before he burst into the national consciousness in 1929 when he was a key witness in the murder trial of Arnold Rothstein, the millionaire gambler who was indelibly linked to the Black Sox World Series scandal of the previous decade. Thompson had set up a sting, and had already fleeced Rothstein out of half a million dollars when the New York gambler became suspicious. During the subsequent confrontation Thompson's sidekick George McManus shot Rothstein. Initially implicated, charges were dropped against Thompson when he agreed to testify for the prosecution against McManus. Needless to say, both McManus and Thompson were acquitted when Thompson lost his memory on the stand.

By the time that trial finished, Thompson was known throughout the States as a gambler extraordinaire – but also as a hustler and golfer of staggering quality, not to mention a man who would cheat and kill without compunction. A famously good player, Ti had won $20,000 in one day through his left-handed scam – he could shoot under 70 left or right-handed and after he'd lost right-handed, would play for ten times more left-handed – and was coming out of the casino when his caddie tried to rob him. Thompson shot him through the heart with the .45 he always carried: 'It wasn't a lucky shot, Ti was an extraordinary shot' said Damon Runyan.

There were other golfing scams (he once bet that he

could drive a ball 500 yards 'if I had to', and then smacked a ball backwards off the tee across a frozen lake) but on the whole he was a player of enormous skill, one who made a fortune on the back of his ability to chip a golf ball into a glass of water from 15 feet every time. He had accomplices such as Lee Elder (the first black man to play in the Masters) and Ky Laffoon, but no one doubted his skill, not least 1944 USPGA champion Bob Hamilton and Byron Nelson, both of whom lost small fortunes playing against Thompson. Yet once asked if he would ever turn pro, he replied, 'I couldn't afford the cut in pay.'

Thompson had other tricks – he could launch fifty-two cards in a row into a hat from twenty feet – and he was a master scammer. His favourite was to bet he could throw a peanut over the clubhouse (he'd loaded the peanuts with ball bearings beforehand). He once encountered a truck loaded with water-melons just outside his home town and paid the driver to unload and count his load: then he bet his fellow drinkers in town that he could guess how many melons were on the truck that had just arrived. Another famous scam involved moving a 'Joplin, 20 miles' road sign in Missouri by five miles in the dead of night and then coming back the next week and betting that it wasn't really twenty miles to Joplin.

ANDREAS KRIEGER

The guinea pig

A famous American anti-drugs campaigner, Dr Bob Goldman, conducted a poll of 100 American Olympic athletes,
asking the question: if someone offered you an undetect-
able way to win an Olympic gold medal, even though it
will kill you five years later, would you take it? Staggeringly, well over 50 per cent said that they would.

Andreas Krieger knows what happens if that Faustian
pact becomes a reality. The 1986 European shot-put
champion and a star of the Communist system, the East
German no longer cuts the startling figure he did 20 years
ago. For a start, he didn't have the three-day stubble back
then, and nor did he have the Adam's apple or the short
hair he now has. In fact, back then, he wasn't a he at all:
Andreas was a girl called Heidi.

Although the West had more than its fair share of drugs
cheats – men like Ben Johnson and women like Florence
Griffiths-Joyner, who died of an abnormally enlarged
heart aged while still in her thirties – Krieger is just one
of an estimated 10,000 East German athletes who were
willing to take vast amounts of drugs from an early age
in order to win Olympic glory. It worked, with the tiny
country winning 384 Olympic medals between 1972 and

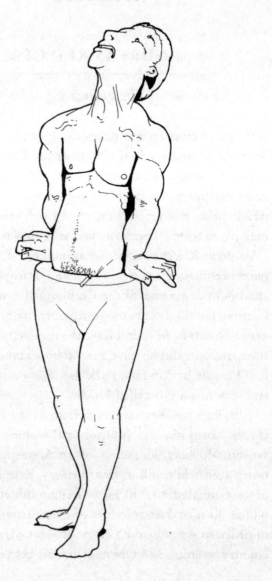

1988, but the price has proved a heavy one for Krieger. In 1997, seventeen years after she first gobbled down a batch of little blue anabolic steroid pills filled with twice as much testosterone as the 'crazy' regime of Ben Johnson, she underwent sex-change surgery.

After starting the regime as a 16-year-old at the Stasi-run Dynamo sports club in Berlin, Krieger's spine is now so damaged that the vertebrae have been permanently deformed, with the muscles and joints also ruined. Every three weeks Krieger needs to be injected with massive doses of the male hormone testosterone or his body goes into shock. 'If I miss one of the shots I soon know about it,' says Krieger. 'My beard stops growing and my body starts going berserk. I am irritable, I cannot concentrate and I frequently burst into tears. It's my body saying it can't cope. I still need these injections to stay male.'

'I thought nothing about the pills, I was only 16. I was ambitious, and besides, everyone else was taking them,' says Krieger, who was soon fancying women and finding herself being insulted in the streets by passers-by, one of whom told her that she 'looked like a drag queen'. She once even tried to kill herself.

Doping at that level was madness, a short-term fix which has wreaked long-term havoc. The American athletes who answered Goldman's question about winning Olympic gold were youngsters who were obsessed with success, but it's broken bodies like Krieger's which live with the results of the craziness.

JOHN DALY

'It's been a four-wheel drive, baby'

In the land of the bland, John Daly sticks out like a sore thumb. Golf may not have anywhere near its fair share of big characters, but the blue-collar mullet-headed hero from Arkansas has waged a one-man campaign aimed at ensuring that as many vices as possible are represented in golf's pitifully small hall of shame. There have been the suicide attempts, the stints in rehab, the benders, the gambling debts, the hotel trashings, the air rage, fighting with opponents' parents, fighting with officialdom, fighting with the police, fighting with his wives. There's even been an autobiographical album entitled 'My Life', featuring cameos from golf-loving musicians Darius Rucker and Willie Nelson. As the self-styled Wild Thing so aptly put it: 'It's been a rocky road. It's been a four-wheel drive, baby.'

Even before he sprang into the public's consciousness with an unlikely USPGA win at Crooked Stick, Indiana, in 1991, Daly had already set about establishing his credentials as a shambling, weak character with a troubled future ahead of him, enduring his first whisky 'overdose' while still at college. Just how troubled, few could have guessed. He has been hospitalised three times for alcohol poisoning, come through two suicide attempts, three divorces, plus countless hotel room trashings and tour suspensions. 'My problem was that when I played bad, I'd go and get drunk. I'm a hell of a competitor; can't stand to play so bad.'

His sponsors Callaway were paying him $3m a year and were desperate to keep the biggest draw behind Tiger Woods on the straight and narrow. Not only did they pay off $1.7m in gambling debts, but they also made him attend AA meetings and hired two psychologists to tame Daly's demons. That wasn't an unqualified success, however; in fact, it was a disaster – they put him on a toxic cocktail of anti-depressants including Lithium, Prozac, Xanax, Paxil, and watched as his weight ballooned to almost 20 stone. Worse still, the side-effects included 'shakes, chills and random craziness' that culminated with a sort of nervous breakdown. Figuring he might as well be hung for a goose as for a gander, Daly fled to Caesars Palace in Las Vegas where he dropped $150,000 on the slot machines. At least it beat the $500,000 IOUs he would litter around Las Vegas later in his career.

Daly clearly has an addictive, needy personality. He still smokes ninety filter-less Marlboros a day, and says he still needs that 'edge', whether it comes from alcohol or gambling. Even keeping his consumption of the Real Thing to reasonable limits has become a struggle: since giving up alcohol he has gone through a dozen big bottles of Coke a day. Yet after a rollercoaster ride that has seen him win two majors and several million dollars, but lose three wives, and saw him arrested for domestic violence and for a confrontation with a flight attendant on a New York-bound plane in Denver, the Wild Thing is in check, for now at least.

STEFANO MODENA

Unlucky for some

There has never been a shortage of superstitious racing drivers. David Coulthard always gets into his car with his right foot first from the left-hand side of the car; Alexander Wurz wears a red boot on his left foot and a blue boot on his right foot; Nigel Mansell would never let anyone touch his crash helmet before a race; and Jacques Villeneuve has two super Mario cartoon men on his dashboard for luck, one saying 'luck' and the other saying 'fuck'. When Michael Schumacher won the world championship in 1994 and 1995, all the mechanics had to wear underwear in which they'd been lucky in, er, love.

But of all the nutty exponents of Formula One (and there are plenty more), none comes close to challenging former Brabham and Tyrell driver Stefano Modena on the superstition front. The wild-haired, bright-eyed, scruffy Italian with the unruly shock of black hair was always a bit on the eccentric side – arrogant and aloof actually – and when he joined Formula One in 1988 he brought with him some ludicrously strange beliefs.

For a start, he had to get into the car from the same side, and then there was an arcane ritual of putting on every piece of his equipment – the balaclava, the helmet, the boots – in a strange order known only to himself. If anyone touched him or spoke to him he had to get out of his car and start all over again. He even wore his fireproof gloves inside out because he believed that he would never win a race if he couldn't see the seams. Not that he ever did win a race, a second-place finish in Canada in 1991 proving the height of his achievement during a decidedly moderate career.

As a footnote, at least Modena didn't follow the example of Argentine goalkeeper Sergio Goycochea, who had possibly the most bizarre superstition outside of tin-pan alley. No matter where he was, to ensure that Lady Luck was on his side before ever penalty, he would hitch up his shorts and urinate on the grass. He even did it during the World Cup semi-final in 1990 against Italy, although his embarrassed team-mates did form a circle around him to hide him from the crowd. And yes, he stopped that penalty, as he did with most of them.

ROBERT JOYCE

That's fan, as in fanatic

We've all come across them, some of us have even the bad luck to have worked next to one: the dull fanatic who defines his life by his team's fortunes, who has no humility about their triumphs, no sense of humour about their failures. Bad-tempered clashes between testosterone-fuelled supporters of different teams have led to endless batterings, stabbings, and shootings across a multitude of sports around the world, but few fans have ever taken their side's reversal quite as personally as a fan of the Brooklyn Dodgers baseball team, Robert Joyce.

It was 12 July 1938, and the Dodgers had just been beaten by their neighbours and rivals, the Giants. Joyce was in a foul mood, so he headed for a place where he could be sure to get a sympathetic hearing: Pat Diamond's bar and grill at ninth and seventh in Brooklyn, or Dodgers Central, as it was known. He was in luck, with the place packed with locals, including Pat's son William, like almost everyone else in the place a fellow Dodgers fan.

'A toast to the Dodgers!' William shouted at a morose Joyce, who was sitting next to Frank Krug, the bar's solitary Giants fans. As Joyce raised his glass, William continued: 'Whoever first called them bums was right, don't you think Frank?'

'Certainly' said Krug. 'It takes the Giants to show them up as bums, too. Ha-ha! What our guys did to them today! Why don't you get wise to yourself Bob? Why don't you root for a real team?'

According to witness statements chronicled in Frank Graham's estimable *The Brooklyn Dodgers: An Informal History*, Bob wasn't for seeing the funny side. It may have been good honest-to-goodness banter for Diamond and Krug, but the butt of their jokes wasn't laughing. Suddenly, he stood up, his eyes blazing and screamed: 'Shut up you fuckers! You lay off the Dodgers, you bastards!'

They both laughed. 'Why Bob!' said Diamond, 'you don't mean to say that you're mad at us boys do you?'

'Don't be a jerk,' threw in Giants fan Krug for good measure.

'A jerk!' Joyce was hysterical now. 'I'll show you who's a jerk.' And with that he ran off along the crowded saloon bar as the other drinkers jeered and laughed at him.

'Jesus,' said Diamond, 'he's got it bad ain't he?'

Three minutes later Joyce was back, a gun in his hand.

'A jerk,' he said. 'A jerk! Hey!'

With that he shot Krug through the head and, as the older man fell, he plugged Diamond in the stomach, injuring him fatally. As the bartender sagged to the floor with blood welling from his mouth, he clawed at the gaping wound in his stomach and turned to Joyce. 'Jesus, Bob,' he said. 'Looka what you done to Frankie!'

BLAIR MAYNE

A true warrior

Softly-spoken, poetry-loving Ulster lawyer Blair Mayne was only 22 when he was first capped for Ireland and played his last rugby international just after his 24th birthday as the winds of war swept across the continent. By the time the hulking second row enlisted in the Army on the outbreak of war, he had won six caps for Ireland and three for the British Lions on their 1938 tour of South Africa, where his no-nonsense play had established him as one of the top forwards of his generation.

He was also, in the words of fellow Lions tourist Harry Bowcott, 'utterly fearless ... our chief party animal'. Bowcott was a hard, hard man yet he saw no shame in ceding second place on that front to Mayne. 'He and old

Blair Mayne

Bill Travers, the Welsh hooker who was a very tough boy too, would put on seamen's jerseys, go down the docks in Cape Town, wait until someone would say something rude about them and then demolish them!' laughed Bowcott. 'That was their idea of a night out. Blair was the heavyweight champion of the Irish universities. Magnificent physique, and a very quiet fellow you thought wouldn't hurt a fly – until you saw him roused. Mad as a hatter.'

Tales of Mayne's hard-drinking escapades are legendary. He wrecked one hotel room with his bare hands in less than two minutes for a bet. Another time, drinking at the bar on that tour of South Africa while dressed in white tie and tails, he got chatting to some South African farmers and was invited out to go and shoot some Springbok. Not one to take no for an answer, Mayne insisted they all went *that very second*. He returned at daybreak (almost) sober, with an antelope hanging around his neck and dripping blood all over his waistcoat. He then proceeded to go looking for his close friend, wing Jimmy Unwin. When he found him fast asleep he just lifted the sheets and tipped the poor beast in alongside the snoozing Englishman.

Yet the characteristics that made Blair a party animal and brilliant sportsman in peacetime also made him a one-man wrecking spree when war came – SAS founder David Stirling called him 'a fighter of satanic ferocity'.

Stirling first came across Mayne in prison, where he was languishing after walloping a senior officer, and immediately recognized a kindred spirit. He wasn't wrong: the Irishman went on to win the DSO and three bars, the Croix de Guerre and Legion d'Honneur, making him the most decorated man in the SAS's history. When Stirling was captured, Mayne commanded the SAS with such success that at one stage 10,000 Germans were employed searching the desert for him.

Yet gongs and statistics alone don't do him justice. Colleagues talk of him 'looking for some good killing' as he departed on various raids, most of which he approached with the same lunatic tactic of racing headlong through German lines in armoured vehicles with machine guns blazing. Mayne was always to the fore, his biggest tally for one day's work being the twelve Germans he gunned down when he single-handedly stormed an officer's mess, plus the forty-seven planes he also destroyed that day. So strong was his rage that when he ran out of fuses to blow up the final Messerschmitt, he ripped apart the cockpit with his bare hands.

The list of suicidal missions undertaken by Mayne in North Africa, Italy, and France is too long to list here, but they all featured an utter disregard for his own safety and an explosion of his volcanic temper. Yet living an adrenaline-fuelled life for six years took its toll. Despite the adoration of the people of his home town of Newtonards, he found readjusting to civilian life a daunting proposition and died in a motor accident on 15 December 1955.

Mayne is just one of several rugby players who exhibited exceptional bravery during the Second World War – Irish internationals Robert Johnston, Thomas Crean and Frederick Harvey, all from Wanderers in Dublin, and Arthur Harris of United Services Portsmouth won the Victoria Cross – but then 203 rugby internationals from the seven 'allied' nations have been decorated during wartime. Rugby's most celebrated VC is former Welsh Rugby Union president Sir Tasker Watkins who, as Lieutenant Watkins of the 1st/5th Battallion Welsh Regiment, single-handedly charged and captured German machine gun positions on three separate occasions on one day in Normandy in 1944.

WADE BOGGS

Mad for It

If you laid all of the over-sexed sportsmen in American history end-to-end, my guess is that they'd reach all the way to Mars and back. Several times over.

My favourite deviants are New York Yankees pitchers

Mike Kekich and Fritz Peterson, who swapped wives in 1973. They traded their wife, youngest child, and dog, keeping their oldest child and house. Kekich's marriage lasted one year and his career nosedived, while last time anyone looked, Peterson's was still going strong.

Other strong contenders include former LA Dodgers great Steve Garvey, who was divorcing his wife to marry his mistress while simultaneously fighting two paternity suits from former lovers. Or there's basketball legend Wilt Chamberlain, who insisted he'd slept with over 10,000 women in his career (that's 1.4 a day!). And then there's the grim philanderer, aka married Houston Astros out-fielder Cesar Cedeno, who was in a Dominican Republic motel room with a teenage girl in 1973 when she was shot and killed during horseplay with his .38 pistol. 'Apparently the case hasn't affected him too much emo-tionally, and that's what's important,' said Astros general manager Spec Richardson of Cedeno's $100 fine for manslaughter.

But of all those Americans with testosterone overload, the case of 'sex addicted' Wade Boggs is probably the most comic. The Red Sox third baseman was, in every possible sense, mad for it.

Most of the time, he had 'it' with Margo Adams, a spurned mistress who revealed that Boggs had 'the libido of a goat'. It turns out that America's finest took his mistress on sixty-four road trips with the team in 1984 alone, insisting that she turn up at games without any underwear. It all started to go wrong, however, when Boggs, who also had countless other flings, ditched Adams after four years of good harmless bump 'n' grind.

So far, so bad, but when Boggs' team-mates told Adams of his new liaisons – they were getting their own back on him for bursting into their rooms and taking pictures of them with ladies who weren't their wives – she did what all good bunny-boilers do: sued him for $6m, appeared in the pages of *Penthouse* and shed some unwanted light on a condition of his that Boggs himself told her that his doctor had diagnosed as 'sex addiction'. Forced to confess to his wife, she agreed to stand by him if he underwent treatment for what he called 'my madness'. They are still together.

ROMANIAN FOOTBALL TEAM OWNERS

What can I get for two bags of ice-cream powder?

If you're looking for comic relief in European football, look no further than the owners of Romania's football clubs. They're not so much barking as howling at the moon. Witness the 2005 transfer window, when second-division Bihor Oradea sold former Steaua Bucharest striker Adrian Negrau to Hungarian outfit Kispest Honved for three televisions and 100 cans of beer. Striker Adrian Vancea was even less highly regarded by Bihor, who sold him to Videoton for 100 beers and two bags of ice-cream powder.

Virtually worthless players clearly abound in the Balkans. Defender Fani Vrinceanu moved from Spartac Posta Cilnau to third-division Olimpia Rimnicu Sarat in return for one pig, while the flash harrys of second-division Tirgu Mures sold midfielder Florin Miclea to Soda Ocna Mures for 200 kilos of meat (unspecified) and 100 litres of wine (red). Defender Virgil Lup made the opposite trip after Soda had handed over 1,000 young trees and a pig. Most embarrassed of all was ASA Tirgu's Florin Dimbian, who was traded to FC Baia Mare for an HGV packed with eggs.

Madness abounds in Romania. Gheorghe Stefan, the nightmarish owner of Ceahlaul Piatra Neamt, assaulted a linesman who made a tough call against his club. When that got him hauled before the Romanian FA he tried to slug president Dumitru Dragomir.

If Stefan was half-mad, Romanian manager Florin Halagian is the full biscuit. A feared disciplinarian whose arrival at any club is quickly followed by an exodus from it, one of his favourite tricks was to drop players who'd

messed-up in the game in the middle of nowhere and make them walk home.

Final proof of the nuttiness of Romanian authority figures comes with the tale of Dinel Staicu, a Ceausescu apologist who bought Universitatea Craiova and promptly sacked six players. Or at least they presumed they'd been sacked – he simply gave them envelopes containing one-way rail tickets to Bucharest. His motivational tactics included getting the players to change in the open air to 'generate team spirit', while he threatened to make players attend a classical music concert if they didn't win a match against Petrolul Ploiesti.

Obsessed with Ceausescu – he was an officer in the militia and runs a theme park and museum dedicated to the former dictator – Staicu recently said he was fed up with football and wanted to start a private jail instead. The 200 masked fans who battled with Universitatea Craiova's security staff would certainly be happy to see the back of him, as would former player Adrian Mititelu, who said of Staicu: 'It's like he wants to enter the legends of Craiovan football as the craziest person ever seen.'

BILL TILDEN

Glad to be gay

If Jack Johnson was one of the bravest black men in America in the first half of the century, then American tennis legend Bill Tilden was his equally brassy gay equivalent. Looking back, it is difficult to know which would have borne the heaviest burden, so reviled were both minorities by mainstream white society. Yet as Johnson bucked the trend with commendable lunacy, Tilden also proved himself just as loud, proud, and stubborn as mad Jack.

His outspoken views and his reckless flaunting of his homosexuality – he would wear body-hugging camel coats on to court and was accompanied at all times by young ballboys – scandalised his contemporaries. Yet perhaps the strangest moment of his career – the one that truly captured Tilden's difficulty with living in his own skin – happened on British soil, at Wimbledon.

It was 1921 and Tilden had already started on a winning streak that was to see him unbeaten in the US Open or Wimbledon for six years. In the final that year, he met Brian 'Babe' Norton, a young South African who idolised the good-looking, dapper Tilden. In awe of each other, and with a scarcely concealed frisson of sexual tension

Bill Tilden

between the two men, both tried to lose the match. Norton clearly threw the second and third sets, and missed several easy passes to win the fifth. The South African even ended the match playing left-handed, while Tilden at one stage tried to cede the match to his opponent.

'I have known several connoisseurs who were present,' wrote eminent tennis historian Ted Tinling about the match, 'and all accepted the fact that a psychological, probably homosexual, relationship affected the result.'

That was just one of the three Wimbledon titles Tilden would win, to go with the six US Opens amassed by the original serve-volleyer. Born into Philadelphia's blue-blood elite, he had been marked down for greatness since he had won a national under-15 title aged eight. Rich, stylish and articulate, he didn't disappoint, winning 93 per cent of his games and, after finally turning professional in 1930, amassing the amazing sum of $500,000 in prize money. When, in 1949, he was voted the out-standing athlete of the first half of the century by America's National Sports Writers Association, he comfortably beat Babe Ruth and Bobby Jones to the title.

Yet none of that mattered to his friends or to the tennis establishment when he was caught in a car with a 14-year-old boy in 1946 and sentenced to two years in a prison work farm for 'contributing to the delinquency of a minor'. He only served eight months, but violated his parole when he was accused of groping a 16-year-old hitchhiker.

His framed portrait which hung in the über-posh Germantown Cricket Club was taken down, his cups taken out of the trophy cabinet. Even Dunlop recalled newly minted racquets with his name on them. He had ceased to exist, and when he died alone and broken in a squalid studio flat in Hollywood aged just 60, he had just $88 in his pocket. No one from Philadelphia or the tennis world attended his funeral. Tilden, who once had it all, was a non-person.

WOODY HAYES

Crazy Hayesey, all Buckeyed and Bonkers

America isn't generally known as a land of great derby matches, but one of the great exceptions is the college football game between the Buckeyes of Ohio State and the Wolverines of the University of Michigan, two institutions in neighbouring states. One man, more than any other, encapsulated that enmity, and his name was Woody Hayes. The gridiron coach for the fearsome Ohio State Buckeyes from 1951–78, Hayes was also famous for a volcanic temper and for his catchphrase: 'Without winners there wouldn't even be any civilization'.

Hayes hated Michigan so much that he even refused to use the word, instead referring to it as 'that state up north' or 'that team up north'. Late one night on a recruiting trip in Michigan, Woody's assistant attempted to pull over for petrol. Hayes, who until that point had been dozing, point-blank refused to let him stop. As the weather worsened and the petrol gauge dropped down to the bottom of the red zone, the assistant begged Hayes to let him stop. Hayes erupted. 'No, goddammit! We do *not* pull in and fill up. And I'll tell you exactly why we don't. It's because I don't buy one goddam drop of gas in the state of Michigan. We'll coast and *push* this goddam car to the Ohio line before I give this state a nickel of my money.' They barely made it across the border and sputtered into the first gas station they found in Ohio.

Michigan wasn't the only thing that sent Crazy Hayesey off on one though. One night, when he and his assistants had been watching video tapes until late into the night, his fellow coaches asked whether they could watch the rest of a particular film the next day. The suggestion pushed Hayes over the edge and, after administering a verbal tongue-lashing, he proceeded to punch himself in the head as hard as he could, time and again. He may have sported two black eyes at training the next day, but he got his own way: they spent another hour reviewing the film.

A compassionate man with a sickly sentimental side,

Hayes was nevertheless loved by his assistants. Once, he was holidaying in the Alps when the exam results came out, so he rang the university, only to be told that one of his star pupils was flunking. Hayes went mad. Ordering that the phone was passed to every assistant, he ripped into each of them in turn. 'I can't trust anybody back there! I go away for two weeks and you kill me! I might as well kill myself right here!' he screamed. Back in Columbus the coaches could hear Hayes going berserk. 'I'm gonna kill myself! I'm gonna jump off a goddam Alp!' he yelled. The coaches in the office began chanting softly, 'jump . . . jump!'. The coach on the phone tried to cover the receiver, but he couldn't. 'I will! I will!' Woody screamed back. 'I heard those sonsabitches! Tell 'em I will! I will!' There was then a cracking sound over the phone, and then silence, and the coaches realized that Woody had ripped the phone out of the wall and thrown it across the room.

Hayes hated losing more than anything else in life, and when results went against the Buckeyes no one was safe. He would always throw his hat when angry – that is, if he wasn't destroying his watch or stamping on his glasses. He would throw anything within reach, which usually meant the water jug on his desk (his assistants always made sure it was empty and kept six spares). He even threw a film projector at his assistant coach Bill Mallory on one occasion.

But in 1978, Hayes finally went too far. It was the final of the Gator Bowl against Clemson and opposing linebacker Charlie Bauman intercepted a pass late in the game to snatch victory from the Buckeyes. Hayes went absolutely mental, punching Bauman and then meting out the same punishment to two of his own players. It was no surprise when Ohio State fired him. He went out the way he came in, with a bang.

BOBBY FISCHER

Pawn star

American Bobby Fischer was the greatest chess player that ever lived. With an IQ of 180 and an ego the size of a house, he burst onto the international chess scene in 1957, aged just 14, when he became the youngest ever American champion before becoming the youngest ever grandmaster the next year. That's all the good news. The bad news was that Fischer was as mad as a March hare with myxomatosis.

By 1962, Fischer complained that he had 'personal problems', and had begun to take a fanatical interest in the quack radio ministers who were gaining in popularity at that time. In particular, he followed a smooth-talking charlatan called Herbert W Armstrong, who co-hosted *The World Tomorrow* programme with his son Garner Ted Armstrong. Fischer was hooked, sending them tithes and buying into their prophecies, including the one about a Third World War between the USA and the United States of Europe.

The corrosive psychobabble spouted by the Armstrongs' Worldwide Church of God quickly turned Fischer's brain to mush. 'If anybody tried to live by the letter of their law, then it was me,' said Fischer. 'I truly tried to be obedient, but the more I tried, the more crazy I became. I can remember times coming home from a chess club at four in the morning, half asleep, half dead and forcing myself to pray for an hour. I was half out of my head, stoned almost.'

For a chess genius, madness wasn't necessarily a problem. The Cold War was at its height and beating the Russians at the game of Lenin, Trotsky and Marx was viewed in the same light as beating the Soviets to the moon. When Fischer earned the right to play the Kremlin's blue-eyed boy, world champion Boris Spassky, the hype was colossal. At one stage Fischer tried to pull out, only to receive a call from Henry Kissinger begging him to play. When the American won 'The Match of the Century', he was the toast of the free world. Yet his mind was going into meltdown.

According to the Worldwide Church of God, 1972 was

supposed to be the year in which the apocalypse ripped the world asunder. Instead, the only one whose world was ripped apart was Garner Ted Armstrong, who became embroiled in a series of tawdry sex scandals. Betrayed by a sect which preached that Anglo-Saxons were one of the ten tribes of Israel, Fischer – himself the son of two European Jews – became a rabid anti-Semite overnight.

Fischer refused to defend his title against Anatoly Karpov in 1975 unless a series of demands were acceded to. When they weren't, he didn't play competitive chess for another twenty years, only re-appearing in 1982 to publish a pamphlet (snappily entitled 'I was tortured in a Pasadena Jailhouse!') detailing his experiences following his arrest in 1981 after being mistaken for a bank robber. His incarceration, so he believed, was masterminded by the international Jewish conspiracy against him.

After that the recluse's mental disintegration was rapid. In 1992, with a $3m fee easing the way, he played Spassky again, but by doing so in Serbia he violated sanctions and had his American passport and citizenship revoked. Railing against New York mayor Ed Koch and US President George Bush – 'who are Jews, secret Jews, or CIA rats who work for the Jews' – he then made sure of his alienation from his former countrymen when he rang a radio station to support the terrorist attacks of 9/11.

'This is all wonderful news,' he told a Philippines radio show as the towers still smouldered. 'It is time to finish off the US once and for all. I was happy and could not believe what was happening. I applaud the act. The US and Israel have been slaughtering the Palestinians for years. Now it is coming back at the US.'

Arrested on his arrival at Tokyo's Nikita Airport in 2004 after twelve years on the run, the scruffy weasel-like figure did his cause little good by punching a prison guard because his egg wasn't sufficiently soft-boiled.

GRAEME OBREE

Cycle of depression

In this collection of eccentrics, lovable loonies, and not-so-lovable nutcases, each of the tales has been designed to bring a wry smile at best, a pained wince at worst. There are even those tales of insane bravery which elicit our admiration – surfer Bethany Hamilton and the Dynamo Kiev team who defied the Nazis spring to mind – yet there is only one Graeme Obree. The term 'madman' covers a multitude of conditions and mental states, but it is generally used as an amused, subjective colloquialism; in Obree's context it is a humourless, objective, clinical term.

Bullied mercilessly as a child on the west coast of

Scotland because his father was the village policeman, Obree developed a deep depression that was to stay with him for the rest of his life. As he said later, even before psychological specialists identified the childhood beatings and head-butts outside the school gates as the cause of his lifelong and untreatable malaise, he grew up believing he was 'a piece of filth'. It was a belief that in many ways defined his life, even when he was the greatest pursuit cyclist in the world.

And make no mistake, Obree was the greatest. In 1993 he came out of nowhere to break Francesco Moser's world hour record with a distance of 51.596 kilometres. Not only that, but he did it with a revolutionary riding style atop Old Faithful, a home-made bike fashioned from the inside of a washing machine and scrap metal the impoverished Scot found alongside the A78. When Chris Boardman broke his record, he rode straight back and broke the Englishman's mark the next year. Then he won the 4,000m pursuit title at the 1995 World Championships despite the fact that the cycling establishment had banned his unconventional riding style. And the Flying Scotsman had public adulation, winning the highly coveted BBC Scotland Sports Personality of the Year award ahead of Colin Montgomerie and Ally McCoist.

Yet a year later at the 1996 Atlanta Olympics, the Scotsman literally had the world at his feet as he stood high on a window ledge contemplating suicide. He had

already tried to kill himself thirteen years before, inhaling acetylene gas in his parents' garage, surviving only because his father had come home early. He had experienced suicidal impulses before, but when his cycle shop went bust in an insurance scam that almost saw him jailed, what the 19-year-old experienced 'was no longer a whim or desire, it was a need, a compulsion'. When his beloved brother Gordon fell asleep at the wheel and was killed by a truck in 1994, it triggered his descent back into the 'black mist' once again.

That mist was particularly dark by 1998, with Obree using alcohol to escape his demons. When he was invited to go to the 1998 World Track Championships as a standby in the team pursuit, his paranoia went into overdrive: the friendlier people were, the more patronised he felt. On the flight back from Australia, he drank so much that he told his team that he would stab them all. If that failed, he said, he would grow a virus and poison them. Back on Planet Earth and half-demented with self-loathing, he chopped his bikes into tiny pieces with a hacksaw.

He rallied enough to accept an invitation to race against Eddie Merckx, Miguel Indurain, Moser et al. at the Rominger Classic road race in Switzerland, but was plastered by the time his flight reached Geneva Airport. Overwhelmed by depression, he decided to succumb to 'the feeling that I am entirely worthless, that those nearest and dearest to me would be far better off if I was dead, and that there is simply no possibility of light at the end of the tunnel.' Swallowing fifty aspirins in a bar at Geneva Airport, he dropped to his knees in the car park and washed them down with dirty water from a puddle, then put another sixty aspirin in his mouth and swallowed hard. Confused, he tried throwing himself into the Rhone, then attempted to cut his wrists with a penknife, before finally breaking into a car looking for a length of seatbelt with which to hang himself. That's when the police arrived, threw him in a cell and sectioned him after he'd finally stopped vomiting bloody mucus.

That Obree's manic depression will be with him for life was demonstrated in 2001 when only the unexpected arrival of a stable girl and his huge lung capacity – six litres instead of the usual two – saved him from successfully hanging himself. But with help from his wife and children, and the knowledge that a reclusive existence is his best chance of a long life, he seems to have reached an equilibrium. He's even written touchingly about his illness and has helped in the production of a £3m biopic based on his life.

MARK BOSNICH

'I've always been a little bit crazy'

Cocaine has ruined plenty of sporting careers, but rarely has there been anything to match the public spiral of decline that marked the end of Australian goalkeeper Mark Bosnich's career. One week he was one of the best shot-stoppers in world football, the next he was failing a drugs test and then holing up with his lingerie-model girlfriend, snorting his way through ten grams a day of finest Bolivian.

Not that Bosnich was ever normal. In fact, he was by his own admission strange: 'I've always been a little bit crazy'. There was, for instance, the time when he threw a Heil Hitler salute (complete with index finger held tastefully under his nose) to the supporters at Tottenham, a club with a sizeable Jewish support. And then there was the time when a tabloid newspaper got hold of his videoed six-some sex romp with team-mate Dwight Yorke and four groupies, an epic production which featured Bozza wearing a dress for much of the tape.

Whether it was momentary marriages, scrapping with the paparazzi outside lap-dancing clubs or checking himself into clinics suffering from depression, Bosnich was football's classic cautionary tale. But at least he knows his own mind. 'If you're going to tell me one night when I'm chatting around four or five girls that I have to be in at 12.30 or one on the dot, then I ain't going to do it. I am no ambassador, I never claimed to be. Only God can judge me.'

With hindsight, it is little wonder that the nutty Aussie eventually fell out with his boss at Manchester United, renowned disciplinarian Sir Alex Ferguson. For a start, Bosnich was a true blue Tory and wasted no time in telling hardman Fergie – a former Govan shop steward who remained red in tooth and claw long after he developed a taste for fine wines and fancy bloodstock – of his admiration for Margaret Thatcher. Sure enough, it all ended in tears.

Moving to Chelsea in flashy west London in 2001 was like leaving a fat kid in a sweetie shop. And Bozza was that fat kid. He gorged on love with model Sophie Anderton, and when he found she was a coke addict, he gorged on the white powder too. Which wasn't altogether clever for someone who once said 'I know I've got an addictive personality.' Quoting Martin Luther King when he said 'life is not worth living unless you find something worth dying for' (we're not sure the great man would have approved of the context) he proceeded to steam towards oblivion.

By the time he failed a drugs test at Chelsea, he was their fourth-choice goalkeeper. Banned for nine months, his cocaine use went nuclear. But the cash soon ran out, followed by the drugs. Then he lost his model girlfriend as well. When Anderton returned for her gear, she instead got into some hand-to-face combat with Bozza, who then fled before being apprehended by the long arm of the law.

Forcibly evicted from his flat by bailiffs working for Chelsea, and absurdly bloated, Bosnich made his last public bow in a charity boxing match against the hard-as-jelly DJ Spoony. That, at least, was one fight he could win.

PETER STOREY

If at first you don't succeed . . .

If you were simply looking for a sporting lag, you could probably choose any one of a thousand men. Whether it's drugs, assault, murder, wife-beating, tax-cheating, or death by drunken driving, jail time and sporting prowess have long been unhappy bedfellows. Yet arguably the most hardened felon in the sporting classes is former Arsenal defender Peter Storey. He may not have the murderous tendencies of, say, a Darryl Henley, but by God he sweeps the board when it comes to criminal persistence.

Storey was actually a pretty handy player, one of the key men in the Gunners' double-winning side of 1971.

Yet Storey's on-field heroics are dwarfed by his off-field activities. As a player living in the same city as Stan Bowles and in the same era as George Best, Storey had good mentors yet never really strayed from the path of righteousness, unless you count the obligatory shagging and drinking that characterized exponents of the Beautiful Game in the Seventies.

As soon as he quit football, however, he quickly established himself as an unlikely criminal mastermind. He was unlikely mainly because everyone on his 'manor' knew him, so when he started up the exotically named Calypso Massage Parlour on east London's glamorous Leyton High Street in 1979, it took the police, oh, about five minutes to work out that it was in fact a brothel. Six months in the slammer and a £700 fine proved to be the shape of things to come.

From there on in, it was an almost continual diet of porridge. In 1980, he financed a plot to counterfeit fake gold coins and was caught trying to sell them on. That'll be three years please. Then, proving that if you try, try again, you can fail, fail again, a matter of weeks after his release in 1982 he was nabbed for running the least efficient car-stealing ring of all time. That'll be another year in chokey then.

Storey decided to diversify, but soon found that high-profile sportsmen-come-master-criminals rarely make effective smugglers. In 1990, coming through customs at

Dover, he was found attempting to conceal twenty 'adult exercise' videos in the boot of his car. For this flagrant breach of the pornography laws, he got a paltry twenty-eight days, which was, completely co-incidentally, exactly the same sentence he got for head-butting a lollipop man in 1999.

STAN COLLYMORE

The madness of King Collywibble

If Stanley Victor Collymore were to be remembered for just one thing, it would be for gifting the word 'dogging' to the English language. Yet English football's twisted genius will be remembered for more than that, so much more. There will be the brawling, the hitting of his girl-friend, the orgies, the drugs, the flirtation with Buddhism, the abortive acting career, the fights with managers. In short, the madness of King Collywibble.

What won't spring to the mind if future generations spare a thought for Collymore will be the fact that when he moved to Liverpool from Nottingham Forest for £8.5m he became the Premiership's most expensive player. Nor will many remember the goals that he scored, not even the winner in Liverpool's 4–3 victory against

Newcastle in arguably the most exciting game of domestic English football. They certainly won't remember that when he retired prematurely at 30 'to let my brain cool down' he was regarded as the biggest wasted talent since George Best.

Nope, if our kids have ever heard of Stan the Man, it'll be because he was, by his own admission, a mad sexual deviant (when he played for Liverpool, opposing fans used to sing: 'You're mad and you know you are'). Deeply disturbed and suffering from clinical depression, his neuroses surfaced in the form of his bizarre relations with women. Even by the standards of footballers he was a prolific womaniser, who was diagnosed as a sex addict and joined SLA (that's Sex and Love Addicts) by The Priory clinic. Just how odd Collymore was became clear to the world when he was caught dogging just outside Birmingham – watching couples have sex in car parks, then joining in. Not that being caught can have come as a complete surprise: although he called himself 'John', he was a household name and turned up in his Range Rover with personalised number plates.

Collymore had already made himself public enemy No.1 when he hit bubbly celebrity girlfriend Ulrika Jonsson in a bar in Paris during the 1998 World Cup. He was fined £500 and bound over to keep the peace after an altercation with estranged wife Estelle, whose house he threatened to burn down and who he threatened to kill. Another of his children's mothers, Michelle, alleged he assaulted her.

Yet things could get worse, and they did when he wrote a warts-and-all autobiography called *Tackling My Demons*. Collymore wrote that he had 'difficulty controlling anger. I have chronic feelings of emptiness and worthlessness. I exhibit recurrent suicidal behaviour. I'm reckless sexually'. But not everybody wanted to hear about it. He claimed that Roy Evans, his coach at Liverpool, was a 'lovely person' and then detailed how he'd slept with his daughter on the night of the 1996 FA Cup; he wrote that Aston Villa first team coach Steve Harrison was the best coach he'd ever worked with, then detailed how the married man visited Birmingham porn shops; he also claimed to have had three-in-a-bed sex with TV presenter Kirsty Gallacher.

That last revelation proved to be a painful one for all concerned. In November 2004, Collymore was drinking in a Dublin nightclub, when he ran into players from Bath Rugby Club, all of whom were friendly with ... Gallacher's boyfriend. With 007 Pierce Brosnan an innocent bystander, Stan started boasting about his exploits with the TV presenter and it all got ugly, with the nightclub brawl ending up with Stan getting a doing in Burger King at 3.30 a.m. When news reports the next day revealed he had a broken nose, bruised rib and fractured elbow, few people shed many tears.

For all that Collymore had mental health issues, it's difficult to conclude anything other than that he was a thoroughly selfish, self-obsessed git. He is certainly guilty on the first charge: when his sister Andrea died from cancer, he didn't attend the funeral because he had booked a holiday in the sun with friends. And he's certainly self-delusional: 'I'm not bad, evil, or a freak,' he said of his dogging episode. 'Everyone has these kinds of problems.'

TED POOLEY

'A madness for easy money'

Long before Hansie Cronje stashed his first wad under the floorboards, betting on cricket was big bucks. The cricket grounds of Victorian England were a magnet for larrikins, ne'er-do-wells, and shysters. In an era when gambling permeated into every facet of life and possession of an untaxed ace of spades was one of the few hanging offences, cricket was almost as important as the racetrack for bookies.

Half the country's bookmakers would have known compulsive gambler Ted Pooley. A gifted wicketkeeper for Surrey it was a testament to his famous charm that he was ever considered for England selection in those priggish days after he was at the centre of a betting scandal in 1873. Suspended by his county for betting on a game against Yorkshire at Bramall Lane, the official minutes refer only to 'insubordination and misconduct', but the real story had Pooley winning a large wad of notes plus two bottles of champagne, which he drank before breakfast, getting so pie-eyed that he was substituted shortly after lunch.

Despite being an inveterate gambler, Pooley was picked by James Lillywhite to be a member of the side which toured Australia and New Zealand in 1876–77, rounding off with the first test match in cricket's history against Australia at the MCG. Pooley should have been playing in that game but couldn't – he was still marooned in New Zealand, where he'd been arrested and put on trial.

Gambling was so widespread in those days that the purses and odds for the major games were published in the local papers, which was too tempting for a man like Pooley, who hit upon a sure-fire way of lining his pockets with little risk. A standard bet was 20/1 to guess the exact score of an individual batsman, so Pooley wagered a huge sum with local Kiwi bookie Ralph Donkin that each member of the Canterbury side would score 0, a common score in those low-scoring days.

Canterbury registered eleven ducks – all of them golden for Pooley, who was also injured so stood as the match umpire (leg before wicket anyone?). When Donkin realized he'd been had, he flatly refused to cough up and a ruckus followed, with Pooley beating the living daylights out of the bookie, loudly informing him that he'd 'have him before breakfast'. He later asked a waiter to tell Donkin that 'if he sleeps in his room tonight he'll find himself half-dead in the morning.'

A week later Pooley and team baggage man-cum-money-handler Alfred Bramhall were arrested, with a Dunedin magistrate fining the wicketkeeper £5 for assault. But Donkin had also laid another charge, that of wilfully destroying property, and Pooley was remanded into custody, with the trial not beginning for another four weeks, by which time the match against Australia had been over for almost a fortnight. It was another three months before he made it back to Blighty, more than a month after the rest of the England party.

Although a man of immense charm – as well as getting off scot-free in Christchurch, the good burghers of Christchurch liked him so much that they had a whip-round which raised £50 and a gold watch – Pooley's reputation was tainted forever. Aged 35, he was never again considered for England duty, he went into a steady decline which only ended when he died a broken bankrupt in a London workhouse thirty years later, ruing 'my madness for easy money'.

TIMMY MURPHY

Rode on the dark side

The world of jockeys is a notoriously hard-drinking one, but few of them drank harder than self-confessed 'moody fucker' Timmy Murphy. As the Irishman said: 'a lot of things can go wrong in racing, and you can be led down paths you don't want to be. There is a dark side. I went down that route and went to the end of it.'

So comprehensive was Murphy's exploration of his dark side that he ended up with plenty of time to reflect on it when he was sentenced to three months at Her Majesty's Pleasure in Wormwood Scrubs in 2002 for what was more of an air-grope than air-rage incident.

This eclipsed even the two-month sentence given to fellow Irishman Paul Carberry in May 2006 when the Grand National-winning jockey was jailed and fined £350 for setting fire to a newspaper on a Spain–Dublin flight the previous October.

Murphy's aberration after he had just ridden Cenkos in the Grand Jump at Nakayama, Japan, and had already chucked down a gallon or two of vodka and orange by the time he arrived at the first class lounge at Narita Airport. Switching to wine, he had lost his memory by the time he boarded the plane back to London. Which is

maybe just as well – first of all he urinated against the doors and walls of the flight deck, then he stuck his hand up a flight stewardess's skirt and copped a feel.

It wasn't the first time Murphy had been in trouble. His first conviction for being drunk and disorderly was five years earlier; a second one, complete with 110 hours of community service, followed in 2001. He had been fired by top trainer Kim Bailey for what the Englishman called 'bad time-keeping'. He was, in short, a hopeless alcoholic.

Even now, Murphy is aware of just how easy it would be to go back to the bad old days. 'I'm a moody fucker and the temper is always there,' he said, 'even if I'm more aware of what triggers it now and I can control it better. My Dad was a rogue. He was always looking for the gamble, looking for the stroke. I could listen to him all night telling stories about the bad things he'd done. There was plenty of skulduggery.' Like father, like son.

GEORGE BEST

Best of times, worst of times

It's difficult to know where to start with George Best, so how about kicking off with what the willowy Ulsterman was originally famous for: playing football. Specifically, he was part of the Manchester United trio of Best–Law–Charlton, possibly the best attacking combo of all time. In just six sublime seasons in the late Sixties and early Seventies he made 361 league appearances for his club, won thirty-seven caps for his country, collected a European Cup and league championship, and was voted both British and European Footballer of the Year. Yet statistics don't do him justice; it was his style and panache which made him a footballing demi-god. Even Pele got in on the act, rating Best the finest player he ever faced, while Britain's sportswriters voted him the best British sportsman of all time.

It says much about Best's subsequent life that his football will forever be in the shadow of his epic philandering, drinking and generally disreputable behaviour. A hopeless alcoholic whose life was defined by his relationship with the bottle, he was so relentlessly reckless that when his obituaries were finally published, being old enough to

claim a bus pass proved to have been almost as much an achievement as winning the European Cup.

Best's drinking started at the height of his fame at Manchester United, when he was receiving 10,000 letters from fans each week, when he was a man about town often referred to as 'the fifth Beatle'. A pliant individual who hated to offend, he'd rarely refuse a drink, which wasn't necessarily the most sensible course for a man with a genetic pre-disposition to booze (his alcoholic mother died aged 56 from the drink and in later life when he had anti-alcohol stomach implants, Best would challenge himself to see how much drink he could take before he became physically sick). Along the way there was a cringe-making appearance on *Wogan* when he appeared the worse for wear, drunkenly informing the watching world that 'I love shagging'. At the end, there was a life-saving liver transplant in 2001, before which he promised to give up the booze. In less than a year he was back on the sauce, within two his young wife Alex was filing for divorce for serial infidelity, although she was at his bedside when he died in November 2005.

As former manager Tommy Docherty, himself no angel, said: 'If only George could pass a nightclub like he can pass a ball.' Another of his managers at Manchester United, Wilf McGuinness, gave an insight into Best's life when he recounted how he caught Best in bed (but not resting) before the 1970 FA Cup semi-final replay with

Leeds. 'He had an absolute nightmare,' said McGuinness. 'We drew 0–0 and George had the chance to win it but fell over the ball in front of goal.'

Best was the role model for every red-blooded male. Out every night and most mornings, the good-looking Irishman would later boast of bedding up to seven women a night and the odd one at half-time, while the bed-post notches contained quality as well as quantity, including four Miss Worlds. But his lifestyle was incompatible with that of a professional sportsman, and aged just 27 he was sacked by Manchester United for excessive drinking and persistent failure to attend training and matches.

From there on, his descent into the Stygian depths was rapid and unhindered. He hawked his talent around a succession of increasingly minor teams (Stockport County anyone?), while off the field he reached a nadir in 1984 when he spent fifty-four days in Ford Open Prison after being found guilty of drink-driving, assaulting a policemen and jumping bail. Regular arrests for drunkenness, drink-driving and brawling punctuated the rest of Best's life, but he seemed to be sublimely unconcerned by any opprobrium, once quipping that 'I spent a lot of money on booze, birds and fast cars. The rest I just squandered.'

Best's tragedy was that he always thought the most famous story about him – a waiter bringing champagne to his hotel room found him with £25,000 of casino winnings scattered around the room and with a semi-naked Miss World in his bed, and asked 'oh George, where did it all go wrong?' – was amusing rather than that spookily prescient. But then the maestro always had a dark side. 'I was born with a great gift and sometimes with that comes a destructive streak,' he said. 'Just as I wanted to outdo everyone when I played, I had to outdo everyone when we were out on the town.'

ROY KEANE

Roy rage

The snarling, raging heart of Alex Ferguson's Manchester United midfield, English football has never known a more ferocious competitor than hard-drinking, hard-tackling Irishman Roy Keane. 'I have this image,' he said, 'the robot, the madman, the winner'. And no wonder: the white heat of his disdain for those who don't share his almost pathological desire to win is spread widely around, and extends in equal measure to 'spivs, bluffers, bull-shitters, hangers-on, media whores, and bad actors'.

A hardman whose working-class childhood in Cork ('a superiority complex is the mark of a sound Corkman' he once half-joked) shaped his outlook on the world, Keane has a relentlessly aggressive, confrontational view of his environment. You sense that he would rather have pursued his career as a promising boxer if only because it would have answered his need for there to be a winner and a loser. 'Boxing is the best sport in the world,' said Keane. 'It's man against man. You're on your own. There's only one person going to come out of that ring a winner.'

Not that Keane needed a ring to get it on. At Nottingham Forest, as a young man uncomfortable in his own skin and not enjoying living in England, he would leave for Cork directly after Saturday's game, arriving in time 'for last orders at the Temple Acre, then a meal with my mates. Saturday was dancing, drinking, kebabs ... Monday, Tuesday and Wednesday, same routine. The amount of fights I've had in Cork that I haven't even mentioned. That would probably be another book. I mean, people go on about my problems off the field, but they don't even know the half of it.' Only his arrest after another brawl in a city centre club, which led to manager Alex Ferguson being summoned to a police station in the early hours just four days before the FA Cup final and ten days before the European Cup final, finally persuaded him to curb a drinking habit that had become a problem.

There are two incidents which prove beyond all doubt Keane's credentials for inclusion in this hall of infamy.

The first concerns his career-ending tackle on Manchester City midfielder Alf-Inge Haaland, the player whose tackle sidelined Keane for the majority of a season. That was bad enough, but Haaland also stood over a prone Keane suggesting he was exaggerating the injury. When the two players next met, Keane was red-carded (one of ten in his career) for a staggeringly reckless lunge. 'I'd waited long enough. I fucking hit him hard. The ball was there (I think). Take that you cunt. And don't ever stand over me again sneering about fake injuries.'

Asked later whether he ever regretted the tackle, Keane said simply: 'No. Even in the dressing room afterwards, I had no remorse. My attitude was "fuck him". What goes around comes around. He got his just rewards. He fucked me over and my attitude is an eye for an eye.'

That much became clear with the second defining moment of Keane's career, his apocalyptic fall-out with Republic of Ireland manager Mick McCarthy at the 2002 World Cup in Japan and Korea. Keane and McCarthy had clashed when Keane was a young member of the Ireland team captained by McCarthy, and in Korea the midfielder was unimpressed by Ireland's 'amateurish' preparations. When he told a journalist so, McCarthy, waving a copy of the article in Keane's face, tried to upbraid him at a team meeting. When McCarthy accused Keane of faking an injury to get out of playing against Iran, Keane went nuclear.

'Mick, you're a liar, you're a fucking wanker,' was how the tirade which would divide a country and a team began. 'I didn't rate you as a player, I don't rate you as a manager, and I don't rate you as a person. You're a fucking wanker and you can stick your World Cup up your arse. I've got no respect for you. The only reason I have any dealings with you is that somehow you are the manager of my country and you're not even Irish, you English cunt. You can stick it up your bollocks.'

DARRYL DAWKINS

Chocolate Thunder from the Planet Lovetron

Long before Shaquille O'Neal was making a destructive name for himself in basketball, a 6ft 11in 22-stone monster called Darryl Dawkins became one of only three players to ever come out of High School and go straight into the NBA – where he promptly smashed two backboards in the jersey of the Philadelphia 76ers.

Yet if that is out of the ordinary, it's as nothing compared to Dawkins' other little foibles. For much of his time in the NBA he wouldn't answer questions from journalists unless they addressed him as 'Chocolate Thunder' ('that's Mr Chocolate to you'). Not only that, but according to Choc, he held dual positions as the Professor of Interplanetary Funkmanship and the Imperial Ambassador from the Planet Lovetron. Confusingly, he would change his name sometimes – one week he would only answer to Sir Slam, the next it was Squakin' Dawkin – yet the Planet Lovetron was a constant theme throughout his fourteen years in the NBA.

Dawkins also amused himself by insisting everyone referred to his thunderous slam-dunks by the names he gave them. 'Hello, meet my friends,' he would say of the 'In-Your-Face Disgrace', the 'Cover Your Damn Head', the 'Yo Mama', the 'Sexophonic Turbo Delight' and – his pièce de résistance – the 'Chocolate Thunder Flying, Robinzine Crying, Teeth Shaking, Glass Breaking, Rump Roasting, Bun Toasting, Wham, Bam, Glass Breaker, I Am Jam'. And on it went. And on, and on . . .

The impossible-to-discipline Dawkins left the NBA to join the Harlem Globetrotters in 1989, and, after a period as a recluse after his first wife died of a drugs overdose, he came back to basketball as the coach of the Pennsylvania ValleyDawgs. He had changed little. 'I am a free spirit,' he said. 'I am a fun-loving guy – and that's the same way I coach. We have fun. We talk trash. We run. We dunk. We throw alley-oops.'

However, when referee Lenny Watson swore at a Valley-Dawgs game, Dawkins became so incensed that Watson had to call for a police escort. Asked about the incident, the Chocolate Thunder agreed that the Planet Lovetron was in need of an overhaul. 'We're redoing the south side of Lovetron in all pink, and it's going to be smashing,' said Choc. 'One side is already in rose, the other side is in teal. So if I put this other side in pink, hey, everything looks pretty in pink.' Of course it does.

Perhaps Dawkins should get together with Bill 'Spaceman' Lee, a former Boston Red Sox pitcher who took so many mind-bending drugs that he started talking to aliens while he was pitching. Among other things, Lee ran against President George Bush in 1988 for the fledgling (and there's a reason for that) Rhinoceros Party.

On the subject of alien theorists, spare a thought for would-be Manchester United owner Michael Knighton, who told the world that he'd been abducted by aliens on the M62 and never lived it down.

RIDDICK BOWE

Kidnapper undone by fast food

One of a whole battalion of mad and bad boxers, former world heavyweight champion Riddick 'Big Daddy' Bowe gets a mention in loony dispatches thanks to his behaviour both in and out of the ring.

In the ring, Bowe's eventual record of 42 wins (33 by KO) and one loss hides a whole range of bizarre fights, a ridiculously high proportion of them being decided by disqualification. In 1991, for instance, he somehow won his first major fight when his manager Rock Newman grabbed opponent Elijah Tijery around the neck and literally threw him out of the ring. Unsurprisingly, a huge ruckus ensued. Two years later, it was Groundhog Day as Bowe lost his rematch with Evander Holyfield – from whom he won the title in 1992 – after fan James Miller parachuted into the ring and caused a mini-riot in round seven of a contest that went down in history as 'the fan man fight'. On the comeback trail and fighting Buster Mathis Junior the next year, the bout was abandoned as a no contest when Bowe hit his opponent while he lay on the canvas.

The bizarre nonsense continued. In 1994, he sucker punched Larry Donald twice on the way to getting a 12th-round decision. The next year Bowe and Jorge Luis Gonzalez staged a series of brutal pre-fight press conferences across the country, with their final meeting having to be held behind Perspex glass. Bowe knocked Gonzalez out in round six.

Although he subsequently beat both Herbie Hide and Holyfield (again) in title fights, he was then involved in more shenanigans when he met Andrew Golota in two title fights, both of which were stopped when the Pole was well ahead but disqualified for persistent low blows – six sledgehammers to the nuts which brought swift retribution from Bowe's cornerman, who cracked Golota over the head with a telephone.

Perhaps being punched down-below unbalanced Bowe, or perhaps not. Either way, his behaviour became extremely weird. Just weeks after his second meeting with Golota, a clearly out of shape Bowe tried to join the Marines, changing his mind after four days 'because I'm not good at taking orders'. In 1998, little more than a year later, and with substance abuse issues a concern, he kidnapped his ex-wife and five children from their North Carolina home, apparently intending to drive them to his home in Maryland. His passion for fast food got the better of him, though, and when he stopped off for a McDonald's, his wife was able to alert the police. Any sense of farce soon disappeared when the arresting officers found pepper spray, handcuffs, duct tape, and a knife in his car.

Perhaps the strangest element to the case is the fact that Bowe only got an eighteen-month prison sentence because he backed up the slurred speech with MRI scans that proved he had brain damage. But in 2005, the same slick lawyer that got his sentence reduced in 1998 – Johnny Cochrane, who got OJ Simpson off the highest-profile double murder charge in American history – successfully appealed to get him his boxing licence back after two states had turned him down. Punch-drunk and mentally disturbed – not a good combination.

OLIVER McCALL

Cry, baby

David Remnick once wrote that 'the history of boxing is the history of men who end up damaged', and few have ended up more damaged than Oliver McCall. Coming just after the so-called lost generation of heavyweights – a self-destructive set of drink-soaked or drug-addled former world champions in Greg Page, Mike Dokes, John Tate and Tony Tubbs – McCall had watched their descent into hell during the Eighties. Yet instead of avoiding their mistakes, he succumbed to exactly the same vices that had robbed them of their lives and careers.

On the face of it, McCall's fate wasn't as bad as, say, that of John Tate, the crack addict who half-killed a hobo for $14 and died when the truck he'd stolen lurched out of control, but at least Tate's mind was (almost) intact. McCall shared the predilection for drugs, with a career blighted by three stints in rehab and arrests for disorderly behaviour, but he will always be remembered for a night in February 1997 when he mentally disintegrated in the ring against Lennox Lewis in front of the entire world.

Having been handed a world title shot against Lewis in September 1994, McCall caught the champion with a glorious right, knocking out Lewis. But McCall let the glory go to his head and by the time of the rematch his personal life was a mess. Arrested just the month before in the foyer of a Nashville hotel as a result of using crack, McCall should not have been in Las Vegas that night. That much was obvious when he bounded up to the ring, eschewing the usual tortuously slow walk from the dressing room. His trainer, ex-boxer George Benton, said that the training camp had gone well, although McCall was 'kinda quirky, but then he's always like that.' But what happened in the ring wasn't quirky, it was the boxing equivalent of a car crash.

By the third round his pace had slowed. Mills Lane, a District Court Judge in Reno and the fight referee, said: 'In the third round he got in close and then seemed frustrated, and then he just backed off and put his arms down. I thought he was playing possum but then I saw his lips started to quiver and I thought, "My God, is he crying?"' McCall refused to return to his corner at the end of the round, and in the next round he walked away from Lewis, then returned to his corner in tears. Asked by Lane if he could continue, he shook his head, but was pushed back out by his cornermen. When McCall refused to defend himself, Lane had little option but to stop the fight: 'I guess they'll put me in prison now,' said McCall.

The pre- and post-fight drug tests were both negative, and the next day McCall fronted up to the press alongside a psychiatrist, who said 'I think his mental state is just fine' before whisking him away. That was the end of any meaningful career although, incredibly, in 2006 he is still fighting.

MARTIN FREINADEMETZ

The Terminator

Our Germanic friends aren't really known for their wild living, but Austrian snowboarder Martin Freinademetz – aka The Terminator – spent much of the 1990s trying to change that. A party animal with a reputation for drunken hell-raising, his finest hour was at the Nagano Olympics in Japan in 1998 when he managed to corner the market in bad behaviour.

That in itself was a major achievement given that he was up against two major talents in undisputed world champion Terje Haakonsen and gold-medallist Ross Rebagliati. Haakonsen turned up, took one look at the whole corporate shebang and caught a plane to California to go surfing. 'You look at the Olympics and they're everything opposite of what snowboarding means,' said the boycotting Norwegian. 'I'm for being free and doing my own thing, and not letting some dude's score classify me. I don't want any part of the Olympics. They're too rigid, and run by a bunch of mafiosos, dudes who are totally not fun. I'm totally into fun.' Rebagliati made even more waves, winning gold and then testing positive for marijuana before getting off with a caution on the grounds that he'd never inhaled (passive smoking, don't you know).

Freinademetz entered into snowboarding folklore at Nagano when he had his accreditation revoked and was kicked out of the country after wrecking the computer and switchboard in the reception of the Shiga Kogen Prince Hotel during a riotous late-night party. Not content with trashing the hotel's computer and sundry bits of furniture, he stripped wallpaper from the walls and smashed up a hotel shop before taking one of the hotel's ski mobiles for an unauthorized and high-velocity spin around the car park. The bill ran to several thousand dollars, a sum which Freinademetz's credit card apparently refused to cough up.

The Austrian was unrepentant. 'We had a party, we had fun, something got broken. It's not cool, but it happened and to throw somebody out of the most important sports games doesn't make sense to me.' Unamused Austrian team spokeswoman Manuela Volvoda disagreed.

'He destroyed a lot of stuff,' she said. 'There was serious damage.'

Still, Freinademetz was well worth his gold in mayhem. In another episode he incited a riot at Stratton Mountain in Vermont which was only broken up when a whole squad of police arrived. The Austrian was eventually arrested and had to post bail for $25,000 after being charged with a felony count of aggravated assault on a police officer. In a sport renowned for its parties, he was the ultimate party animal: not only did he race in a gorilla suit, but fights with other snowboarders were commonplace.

It is ironic that he will be remembered for the ruckus at the Olympics in Japan. Not only did he campaign vigorously against snowboarding becoming part of the Olympic family, memorably comparing Juan Antonio Samaranch to Al Capone, but he also held a vigil at International Ski Federation (FIS) races with a banner saying: 'Bomb the FIS headquarters'.

TOMMY MORRISON

The Duke of Destruction

Former world heavyweight champion Tommy 'The Duke' Morrison hopes that his soon-to-be-completed autobiography, *Down But Not Out*, will be turned into a TV movie. It would be compulsive viewing, what's become known as car crash television.

But why stop at one biopic? After all, there has been enough carnage, disaster and destruction in the redneck boxer's life to fill a trilogy. The first instalment could be about the guns, the next could be about the girls, while the concluding episode could be a catch-all containing the drugs, the cars, the organised crime, the disorganized crime, the jail-time, the drunken driving, the steroids, the bare-knuckle fighting, the domestic abuse, and the bosom buddy and partner-in-crime called Bart Bumpass.

Morrison will be remembered as a typical pugilistic basket-case, a man of many arrests and convictions, almost all of them involving cars, guns, drugs, and drinking – and sometimes all four. In committing the crime for which he was sentenced to ten years in 2000, for instance, he was already on bail for previous drugs and weapons charges which included cocaine possession, simultaneous possession of drugs and firearms, being a felon in possession of a firearm, possession of drug paraphernalia, misdemeanour possession of marijuana and driving while intoxicated. And that's without the 1997 conviction from driving under the influence and causing a chain-reaction traffic accident that seriously injured three people, which in turn was simply the latest conviction for what Americans call DUI.

So when a legless Duke was caught hightailing it away from a crashed Corvette containing a large stash of drugs he reckoned he was in trouble. That inkling turned into a certainty when bemused officers found that as well as the handgun Morrison was carrying, his car contained several more weapons of mass destruction, including a .45, two .22s and two .40s, as well as a pump-action 12-gauge shotgun they described as a riot gun. Most of the weapons were equipped with laser sights and all were loaded with armour-piercing ammunition. It didn't help that Morrison had attempted to impersonate a police officer to facilitate his not-so-quick getaway.

The roots of Morrison's madness came in his youth. His mother had stabbed another woman to death, but still she couldn't control the young tearaway, so when he dropped out of school aged 13 he was sent off to live with his father in a trailer in Arkansas. That wasn't a good idea because his father was a hood who, when angry, beat him with a chair, lamp, ashtray or whatever came to hand. The old reprobate soon dragooned his teenage son

into helping him collect extorted money for 'Irish gangsters' and made him fight in tough-man contests – brutal
bare-knuckle fights with no rules.

'I used to think that being a faction of an organized
crime situation was cool,' said Morrison. 'You say, "You
owe this much money and what do you plan on doing?
If you don't pay, I'm not responsible for what's going to
happen to you." I didn't necessarily always have to be
the one to do it, just inform the right people of where
they live, where they hang out, who their friends are,
where their kids are.'

The hard life had a silver lining though. Morrison had
first fought competitively aged eight. He won a Golden
Gloves competition in Kansas City as a senior in high
school and competed in the 1988 US Olympic trials,
before going on to beat George Foreman in 1993 to take
the WBO world heavyweight title.

But his fast living also took its toll, with Morrison
being diagnosed as HIV positive in 1996, shortly after he
was knocked out by Lennox Lewis in the sixth round of
their title fight. Although Morrison believes he contracted
the condition through injecting steroids, it's more likely
to be down to having sex with an 'astronomical number'
of women as part of his training. 'Sex became a part of
my conditioning program,' he says. 'It was just all the
time; three different women a day for seven or eight
years.'

It would be fitting if Morrison's life were made into a film. Not only did he often claim to be John Wayne's nephew, but he starred in *Rocky V* opposite Sylvester Stallone. Predictably, he played a psycho boxer.

LUCIANO 'RE' CECCONI

The King is Dead . . .

If Lazio's fans believed they were cursed for most of their history, who could blame them? The great under-achievers of Italian football, the Rome side's fans had to wait almost a century from their formation until they finally won Serie A in 1974. Few titles have been greeted with more relief or with more genuine delight. Yet nothing lasts forever when you're a Lazio supporter and as soon as that title was in the bag the dream slipped away for another quarter of a century.

The reason for Lazio's swift disintegration after winning the 1974 Scudetto was a bizarre accident that ripped the guts out of the club. Actually, to call it an accident is probably a little inaccurate.

The beating heart of that title-winning Lazio side was a dashing midfield god with pork chop sideburns, flowing blond locks, and a penchant for extreme practical jokes.

Long before Wimbledon's 'Crazy Gang' came on the scene, Luciano 'Re' (or 'King') Cecconi was nailing team-mates' shoes to floors, cutting the sleeves off Armani suits, and generally being a nuisance. An inveterate practical joker and hoaxer, on the rare occasions he was rested he would sit on the bench in a full-length fur coat. Even in the height of summer.

The joke, however, was on Cecconi on a cold winter's day in January 1977 when he tried to amuse a friend with a merry jape that went disastrously wrong. Accompanied by best friend Peter Ghedin, the two men went to visit another acquaintance, jeweller Tawny Tabocchini, who was stressed because he'd been the target of several successful raids by thieves. They planned to take him out for lunch.

Just before they arrived at Tabocchini's shop, Cecconi tucked his giveaway blond hair under his fedora hat and pulled his coat collar up to conceal his face. Putting his head down so that he couldn't be recognized, he burst through the door, and pulled a water pistol out from under his coat. 'Nobody move,' he screamed, 'this is a hold-up!' Unfortunately, the unfortunate Tabocchini wasn't listening – as soon as he saw the gun, the jeweller panicked, reached under the till and pulled out the handgun he now kept there for just such raids. By the time Cecconi's lifeless body hit the ground, it was riddled with bullets.

JOHN KORDIC

Rage, rage against the dying of the fight

Ice hockey's teak-tough enforcer is something of a sporting cliché, yet there was nothing hackneyed about hardman John Kordic. A talented player who ascended to the status of hockey deity when he won a Stanley Cup ring (ice hockey's equivalent of a Superbowl ring and FA Cup-winners' medal rolled into one) with the Toronto Maple Leafs as a 21-year-old in 1986, Kordic gained his pre-eminence because he could – and would – employ as much violence as he needed to physically dominate games. As defenceman Dave Shand once said: 'Kordic might have been the toughest guy in hockey, but he was totally wacko. He'd spear you in the face for nothing.'

Yet Kordic was a man at odds with himself. He needed the adoration that came with a trail of broken bodies, yet he cried at rinkside after his father told him how much he hated the way his son played. His response? To drown his self-doubt and self-loathing in a toxic sea of booze, cocaine and steroids.

Not that his opponents knew of his inner turmoil. All they saw was the naked aggression, unprovoked attacks, steroid rage and blood on the ice. 'He beat the shit out of everybody,' says Jean Perron, his coach in Montreal.

'He was the best fighter in the league. Nobody could take John Kordic. The fans in the Forum would chant his name. Kor-dic! Kor-dic! Kor-dic!'

There was, as Perron admitted, no way that Kordic could quit. The buzz was too intense, the adoration too addictive. 'The only way for him to attract attention was to fight, and he loved the attention,' said Perron. 'After he beat up Gord Donnelly of the [Quebec] Nordiques before an opening face-off in 1988, as he was skating off the ice he kissed his fist and held it up to the crowd. I never saw anyone else do that, before or since.'

Yet Kordic spent as much time off the ice as he did on it. At Washington he logged 101 penalty minutes in seven games. He played nineteen games for the Nordiques and spent 115 minutes in the sin bin. At Toronto in December 1988 he was suspended for ten games for high-sticking the Edmonton Oiler's Keith Action, breaking his nose beyond repair in the process. As Gord Stellick, the Maple Leafs general manager, said: 'He was a walking time bomb that no one could defuse'.

That walking time bomb went off in August 1992. Kordic had been dumped by a succession of clubs after positive drug tests, dropping out of rehab, being arrested for assault and trashing his girlfriend's flat. He was playing for a minor league team but his consumption of nose-candy was of major league proportions as he roared through five grams a day and watched his spending soar to $1,000 a week. He was so wired that his habit caused him to claw frantically at his skin in public.

Pushed over the edge by his father's death and suffering increasingly frequent periods of black depression, the monstrous Kordic – steroids had turned the 6ft 2in 27-year-old into an ultra-aggressive, 18-stone ball of rock-hard muscle – was continually in bar brawls, usually ones he'd started. On 8 August 1992, he booked into the Motel Maxim in Quebec. Staff, worried by his abusive phone calls and smears of blood on the windows, called police. When the Mounties arrived, they found Kordic hitting himself in the face, the room trashed and blood everywhere: it was a classic case of steroid rage.

Kordic had taken a lethal speedball – a bottle of vodka, injection of cocaine into his arm, and an injection of steroids into his butt – and was going mad. By the time nine gendarmes had finally subdued him – using two sets of handcuffs and chains to pin his grotesquely strong arms – he had suffered a cocaine-induced cardiac arrest. Six years after winning the Stanley Cup, Kordic was dead, his legacy forty syringes in a shabby hotel room.

STEVE MICHALIK

The Phantom Menace

One of the most disturbing moments in researching this book came when I encountered aspiring body builder John DeFendis's web diary detailing his time as the protégé of Mr Universe Steve Michalik, the man dubbed by Arnold Schwarzenegger as 'the Phantom'. It's hardly a secret that body building is a pursuit replete with oddballs, and for most people it is a given that the bodies of these outlandishly big men are rarely created without the use of steroids, but the details of Michalik's insane drive to be the biggest and the best were still extraordinary, unbelievable almost.

The most shocking moment in DeFendis's blog was his account of the day when he became Michalik's unquestioning disciple. On the way to the beach, DeFendis asked Michalik what he needed to do to become like his mentor. Without a word, Michalik led his pupil out into the surf and, without warning, dunked him under time and again, until a semi-conscious DeFendis thought he was about to die. 'Tell me how it felt to have one breath,' Michalik screamed at DeFendis. 'How bad did you want that little breath of air? When you want to win as bad as you wanted that one breath of air, then come back and see me. That's what it will take for you to be the best.'

By any standards, Michalik was a 24-carat nutcase. Abused by his parents, he took to body building aged just eight, determined 'to turn myself into Captain America' and prepared to die in the process; (his motto, written in blood red on the black walls of his gym, was 'train beyond the pain ... death is your only release'). He was so obsessed with becoming huge that he went to the extreme of buying monkey skulls, cracking them open and drinking the hormone-enriched fluid that came from the hypothalamus. Even a near-fatal car crash in 1976 which left doctors telling him he'd never walk again didn't stop his obsession: he drove to the gym at 3 a.m. each night, his little brother working the pedals while he steered.

Michalik's steroid consumption was epic. He started taking steroids in 1972 and was soon addicted, taking a cocktail of fourteen different drugs, with 'speed' to get through his workouts and downers so he could get some sleep. At his gym, there was a two-foot syringe above the front desk with a sign which read: 'Message Of The Day: Up The Dosage!' When gym users signed in they did so using a syringe with a pen inserted through it.

The steroids were the only way he could get through an eye-popping, puke-making training regime he called 'Intensity or Insanity', but they took a terrible toll on his body. His ingestion of female fertility drugs such as

Halotestin, Clomid, and HCG was intended to increase his testosterone levels but also gave him a virtually permanent erection and made him sex-crazed. 'I was insatiable, and acting out all over the place,' said Michalik. 'I had girlfriends in five different towns on Long Island, and one day I was so hormone-crazed I fucked them all right after the other.'

Sounds great, right? Wrong. Excessive libido is all very well in theory, but the practical ramifications of testosterone rage are unspeakable if Michalik is to be believed. 'One of my friends, a former Mr America, used to get so horny on tour that he'd fuck the Coke machine in his hotel,' said Michalik. 'Swear to God, he'd stick his dick right in the change return slot, and bang it for all he was worth. He fucked those machines from coast to coast, and even had ratings for them. I seem to remember the Chicago Hyatt's being pretty high up on the list.'

Michalik was huge, but ailing. A decade of shotgunning steroids turned his joints into mush; he was bleeding from his gums, kidneys, colon and sinuses and was pissing blood until one day he instead started pissing brown, pure protoplasm that his failing liver hadn't been able to break down. Eventually his migraines got so bad that the only relief was getting his son to pack his head in ice. He almost died during one competition when he went into spasms on stage.

Although his body was failing and his muscles sagging,

only the death of a close friend – the LA Raiders' football player Lyle Alzado in 1992 from cancer brought on by excessive steroid use – brought Michalik to his senses. Even then he almost didn't make it. His sperm count went to zero, he didn't get an erection in over two years, all the oestrogen in his body turned his pectorals into breasts and his kidneys began to fail – and only a revolutionary detox programme saved him. Now an anti-steroid campaigner and personal trainer for senior citizens, his mantra has changed. 'There is no such thing as good drugs, only bad drugs and sick bastards who want to sell them to you,' he says.

TANK ABBOTT

Anyone, any place, any time

There have been many fighters skirting the edge of reason in the history of organised pugilism, but few characters to match celebrated American streetfighter David 'Tank' Abbott. He has never dominated the Ultimate Fighting Championships – the savage hybrid which pits martial artists, boxers, and kick boxers against each other – but Abbott has become a legendary figure in the most uncompromising combat theatre of them all.

With his motto of 'anyone, any time, any place', the crazed Californian has never shirked a fight, but many fighters have fought shy of facing the teak-tough ZZ Top lookalike with the most compelling statistic in UFC history – 90 per cent of his opponents have ended up in hospital. In UFC, there are few rules: two men go into a fighting pit surrounded by a five-foot high net, one man walks out, and the other is carried out. Simple but brutal. And Abbott, an overweight bar brawler who can benchpress 600lbs, who trains 'on my barstool' and who drapes his T-shirt morgue-style over fallen victims, is as brutal as it gets.

Unlike virtually all of his opponents, Abbott has no martial arts background. He was an All-American wrestler who went bad in his teens, fighting in the streets until he discovered boxing aged 25. Despite being a History graduate, it was the more primeval side of Abbott's nature which triumphed. As he says, once he discovered how much he loved the pain of boxing, he 'just wanted to rip everybody's head off.'

Fighting in his first UFC event in Wyoming, he was listed as a 'pitfighter', but quipped 'I don't give a rat's arse what you call me, just let me fight.' Weighing in at 19-stone, the Tank met the Dumptruck in the shape of 28-stone Hawaiian John Matua, a specialist in the ancient bone-breaking art of Kuialua. Abbot wrecked that vehicle in twenty-one seconds, Matua needing to be helped from the cage wearing a new accessory, an oxygen mask. In his next bout with 22-stone Paul 'The Polar Bear' Varelans, Abbott kneed the 6ft 8in trapfighting expert in the head, ending the fight in less than two minutes. Abbott lost the final against Russian Oleg Taktarov by a choke, but the bout lasted almost eighteen minutes and is still regarded as the greatest fight of all time. 'It was a war,' said Abbott. 'Two guys in a war, and that's what went down. It was a good time.'

But Abbott isn't listed in these pages simply for his feral cunning and animal ferocity in the cage, or even for being the only man willing to fight world champion Maurice Smith at the height of the kick boxer's fame, but for his record as a streetfighter with an unquenchable thirst for violence. He even managed to get in a row when he went to Fremantle to watch the Americas Cup, decking four of the huge grinders – the guys who wind in the sails – before the police showed up and another spell in chokey ensued. Scrapping is just in his blood, he says. 'Those grinders thought they were gonna box me to hell 'til I started using their heads for a soccer ball,' he says. 'Shit, I'm going to be fighting when I'm seventy, if I'm still alive. I mean, that's what I love to do.'

CARLOS ROA

Captain of the God Squad

A surprising number of sportsmen have put God before their careers, including All Blacks flanker Michael Jones, who refused to play in the 1987 World Cup semi-final because it was held on a Sunday, and Eric Liddell, who famously put his athletics career on hold to go and become a missionary in China. Yet neither did so because they believed the end of the world was nigh. But goal-keeper Carlos Roa did.

The Argentine had always been known as an eccentric, hence his nickname of El Lechuga ('The Lettuce') at Racing Club because he was that rarest of beasts in Argentina, a vegetarian. River Plate even backed out of a big-money move for the quiet teetotaller because they had heard he was part of a religious sect, and during a meeting with the club he talked of the imminent arrival of the Second Coming and the subsequent end of the world.

But when the man who had saved David Batty's penalty at France '98 and helped Mallorca to the Cup Winners' Cup final at Villa Park the following year retired in 1999, the full extent of his religious fervour became apparent. Not that it was exactly a secret – he insisted on wearing the No.13 rather than the traditional No.1

because 'the one is for God the creator and the three because Christ rose on the third day.' He also turned down a huge offer from Manchester United, telling Alex Ferguson that 'money isn't everything. God is worth more than $10m.'

With the devout Seventh-Day Adventist refusing to play on Saturdays after dusk, which was proving a tad problematic for his club Real Mallorca, something had to give. And that something happened to be the end of the world. In 1999 Roa did a bunk, disappearing into the Argentine hinterland with his family and brothers, and setting up a phone- and electricity-free commune in the tiny village of Villa de Soto, where he awaited the return of Christ and the subsequent Apocalypse. 'I was a footballer because God had a plan for me,' he explained, 'but I never wanted to be a footballer. I didn't like it and it didn't interest me.'

When 2000 came and went without the celestial Millennium bug turning the world to dust, Argentina team manager Jose Pekerman tried to talk Roa around. 'If he does give me the chance to talk to him, I'm going to teach the Bible to him,' said the saintly one when told of Pekerman's imminent arrival, adding that the only thing he might want from the 'real' world was the chance to be a fighter pilot. He'd always wanted to be a fighter pilot, he said.

Roa isn't the only God-squadder who has put the Lord

before his career. Edinburgh Rocks basketball coach Greg Lockridge famously refused to give court-time to any player who wouldn't pledge allegiance to the Almighty, the screaming ex-US Marine getting the boot after less than two months in the job.

JACK RUSSELL

Mad Dogs and Englishmen

In years to come, when someone gets around to publishing a dictionary of sporting jargon, the words 'cricketing eccentric' will undoubtedly be followed by '(c.f.: Jack Russell)'. The England wicketkeeper was one of the great talents of his generation, yet it can only be a matter of time before the memories of his skill behind the wicket dim to the point where the strange and obsessive personality that drove the high-achieving 'grubby-haired schoolboy from a council house in Stroud' will be all that remain. Well, that and the watercolours he now flogs to the Duke of Edinburgh for £10,000 a time.

Whenever Russell's eccentricity is raised, Exhibits A and B invariably concern his diet and his clothing, but my favourite image of Russell is of the man so obsessed with his privacy that he would blindfold tradesmen and take them on circuitous routes back to his house, criss-crossing the countryside so that they couldn't identify where he lived. Players who he had laboured alongside him for twenty years don't have his address and he even encouraged his five children to make up outrageous stories about his unwelcoming, aggressive behaviour to dissuade visitors.

Russell was almost autistic in his demand for a strict regimen, and nowhere was that more famously displayed than in his diet. Russell's mother confirmed that 'he wasn't an easy child . . . he would go weeks surviving on nothing but oxtail soup and chocolate biscuits', and his regime didn't get any less idiosyncratic as he got older including, as it did, twenty pots of tea every day of the year. His Gloucestershire team-mates knew his match-day routine off-pat: a chocolate biscuit and cup of tea at 10.30 a.m.; tuna, jacket potato, and beans with a pot of tea at 1.20 p.m. When one of his team-mates helped himself to a cup of tea from Russell's lunchtime pot, the unfortunate player was forced by Russell to have a cup at precisely 1.23pm every day for the rest of the season.

When with England, Russell's routine of hanging one tea bag on his dressing room peg to last him a full five-day Test match was legendary, as was his absolute insistence that his two Weetabix should be soaked in milk for exactly eight minutes, but his dietary dippiness would go into fifth gear when he toured overseas. He went through one tour of India eating nothing but a packet of Jaffa cakes per day and an evening concoction of mashed potato, rice, baked beans, and brown sauce. When England toured South Africa in 1996, his excess baggage charge was astronomical because he insisted on taking a suitcase full of tins of rice pudding, baked beans, and corned beef and weighing 80kgs.

His attachment to his mouldy old hat was his other famous foible. He wore it every day for twenty years and under no circumstances would he countenance wearing anything else, even when threatened with being kicked off the Test team. Only his wife was allowed to wash it before drying it on a tea cosy over a biscuit tin to keep its shape.

The moustachioed one was utterly professional and left little to chance (his funeral is already booked, the arrangements to have his hands amputated and preserved in formaldehyde long-since made). A noted sledger of batsmen in the days when the practice was an almost exclusively Aussie preserve, he was also a hugely talented wicketkeeper who played in fifty-four tests, forty one-day internationals, and who took 1,192 catches and made 128 stumpings in first-class matches, scoring 16,861 runs at an average of 30.93. A perfectionist, he kept a diary of every ball he ever faced and took failure very badly: in South Africa in 1996 he locked himself in his room for two days as punishment for dropping a catch, and he once had to be physically restrained to stop him jumping from a fifth-floor Guyana hotel balcony when his standards dipped below his own expectations.

An outspoken opponent of wives touring with the team ('Wouldn't take your missus to the office, would you?' he'd ask), his one self-consciously eccentric demand was to have 'How Much Is that Doggy in the Window?' as his theme tune in one-day matches. His 23-year career ended in typically singular style when he slipped a disc reaching for the *Racing Post*.

ALAIN ROBERT

Super fly guy

Are people who do crazy things necessarily mad? Does someone who enjoys the thrill of drag racing or the rush of sky-diving or the cave-diver who likes to explore deep into the earth's hidden recesses qualify as unhinged unless they push themselves beyond their own personal comfort zone? For the purposes of this tome we've assumed not, otherwise we'd have a book full of extreme athletes of indistinguishable character, with their only claim for inclusion their ability to go higher, faster or further.

That said, there's always one exception, and that

exception is Frenchman Alain Robert, aka Spiderman. Perhaps it's because I suffer from vertigo (poor lamb), or perhaps it's because Robert is the only solo extreme climber ever to have navigated his way up the smooth surfaces of the world's highest skyscrapers, but his feats are scary both in planning and in execution. Not only that, but where base jumpers have a fair to middling chance of getting away before the forces of law enforcement hove to, the same doesn't apply to Robert, who can expect to find the local constabulary waiting for him at the end of his journey.

That, though, doesn't make him insane. The 5ft 5in climber clinches that status by conquering over seventy major buildings around the world – including Canary Wharf, the Eiffel Tower, the Empire State Building, and the Petronas Towers in Kuala Lumpur, where he was arrested when he reached the sixtieth floor – with his bare hands and feet *without the use of any form of safety device*. And it's not as if he hasn't known the pain of failure. Robert started climbing buildings as an eight-year-old when he was locked out of his parents' eighth-floor apartment, and in one accident-prone year as a 19-year-old he suffered two 15-metre falls which left him needing nine operations, fractures to his wrists, heels, nose, both forearms, elbow and pelvis. After the second fall he was in a coma for five days, with doctors telling him he may never walk again, let alone climb.

Alain Robert

Since honing his skills in the French Alps, the elfin figure's finest day was his successful hour-long ascent of the 1,450-ft high Sears Tower in Chicago, a feat he still counts as his most dangerous after dense fog at the ninetieth floor of the 110-floor building made the windows on the remaining twenty floors dangerously slick. On three separate occasions he almost lost his grip and slipped to his death. His highest-profile climb was of the 656-ft National Bank of Abu Dhabi, which was conducted in front of over 100,000 onlookers in 2003.

ADA KOK

Wife from hell

To aficionados she remains the best butterfly specialist of all time. In the record books Dutch swimmer Ada Kok (great name, great woman) will be forever remembered as the first female Olympic 200m butterfly gold medallist after she won the inaugural event at the distance at the 1968 Mexico City Games before going on to become, among other things, a double Olympic silver-medal winner, the European champion, the holder of ten world records, and the two-time European Swimmer of the Year.

To everybody else – especially her long-suffering husband, Matt Van Der Linden – she will be remembered as an utterly mad, if lovable, eccentric. Her husband bore the brunt of that eccentricity: she once sold his car to a passing gypsy and bought some new glasses with the money. Another shocking example of her rejection of material values (or at least her husband was shocked) came when he was decorating the house. As it was a sunny day, she told him to move the furniture out onto the lawn while he got on with the painting. Legend has it that she sold the lot, although she swears that she merely failed to stop passers-by walking off with their possessions.

Kok was a girl of commendable high spirits. When she won her first gold medal in Mexico City (after winning her first European title aged 15 she had won two silvers in Tokyo in 1964) she celebrated by sneaking into the Dutch ambassador's bedroom at a buttoned-up post-Games party and spending an hour bouncing on his bed to win a $100 bet – all very well until the startled ambassador walked in, catching her in the act. She partied so hard after winning the gold that she ran into the Dutch Olympic team's chef de mission on the way back into her hotel the next monring. Only some frenetic lobbying by team-mates stopped her getting sent home on the first plane out of Mexico City.

DON KING

Teflon Don

Twisted genius Don King is like PT Barnum crossed with Joseph Goebbels and then sprinkled with a pinch of Sam Goldwyn. A Shakespeare-spouting maverick showman with few friends, no conscience and a limitless lust for greenbacks, the two-time killer has bestrode the heavyweight division of world boxing for thirty years, using a mix of ruthless cunning, low tricks, blatant intimidation and endless charm to consolidate his iron grip on the sport. As a pugilistic bogeyman he has no equal. As King says: 'If I didn't exist, you would have had to invent me.'

As a youthful numbers runner in Cleveland, grossing $10,000 a week, he and the law were on nodding terms early in his life. Arrested thirty-five times between 1951 and 1966, his 1954 shooting of a would-be burglar was dismissed as justifiable homicide, but when he punched, kicked and pistol-whipped Sam Garrett to death in the street in 1966 over a $600 debt – the last words King's former friend said were 'okay, okay, you'll get your money, Don' – he was jailbound. Even then, inexplicably King's life sentence was commuted to involuntary manslaughter. He served less than four years.

King's entrée into boxing was through rock 'n' roll

legend Lloyd Price, who knew both King and Muhammad Ali (Price was the man who recommended King comb his hair upwards 'to make you memorable'). When King managed to get Ali to show up at a benefit fight night for a local hospital, he got his claws into the champion and never let go. His graduation was the Rumble in the Jungle between Ali and George Foreman in Zaire in 1974, his passing out parade the day in 1978 when he got Leon Spinks stripped of the heavyweight crown he'd won against Ali thirty-one days before.

After that, aspiring heavyweights knew they had to be in King's stable to qualify for a shot at a world title. His absolute power was augmented by brazen use of the race card and his charm offensives. Stories about him rushing across the ring and stepping over one of his vanquished fighters to sign up the victor are legion, but my favourite King yarn concerns his attempt to get Greg Page to sign to his stable. At the funeral of Page's father in 1982, King arrived at the church weeping and threw himself into the grave to land on top of the coffin before being helped out, dusting earth from his suit. King left an hour later with a signed contract. 'It happened so fast,' said Page, 'the doors opened and there was Don, smiling his smile.' It happened with Mike Tyson too: he was signed up at manager Mike Jacobs' funeral. King had a talent for getting fighters when they were at their weakest.

King always got a better deal than his fighters. Often

financially illiterate and blinded by the desire for a shot at the title, they found themselves fleeced by a management fee of 50 per cent plus deductions. Tim Witherspoon's $1m purse for his 1986 title defence against Frank Bruno, for instance, left him with $90,094 after fees and 'expenses'. Some fought back – Mike Tyson sued King for $14m, Terry Norris got $7.5m, and Ali sued him for $1.2m – but despite over 100 writs, those boxers who got money back were rare exceptions. As King said: 'The ultimate gravitational force of the universe is money, baby. It ain't all this brotherhood'.

In his coruscating *Only in America: The Life and Crimes of Don King*, biographer Jack Newfield asserts that King accepted $1m from South Africa's apartheid regime during Nelson Mandela's boycott. Other allegations against King include ruining boxers' lives, careers, and spirits, betraying friends, instigating racial conflicts, and enticing an ailing Ali out of retirement to face Holmes and endure the worst beating of his career.

King seems to have led a charmed life. There have been a number of investigations that have failed to turn up enough evidence to convict him of any offence, and such is the chutzpah of the ageing promoter that the only thing he thinks is worse than people's damning opinions of him is them having no opinion of him. So here, for the record, is what they say about the mad, bad Machiavelli of the street.

'Forget death and taxes, the only sure thing is that, win or lose, Don King is counting the money' – biographer Jack Newfield.

'He really uses money as a form of power and control over fighters. I believe that deep down Don hates fighters, is jealous of them. That is why he wanted to have such power over us, to humiliate us. When I see Don, I see the devil. The reason he wears his hair so funny is to hide the horns' – King fighter Larry Holmes.

'You don't understand. Don King *is* organized crime' – Ali biographer Thomas Hauser when asked by a Senate committee if King was linked to organized crime.

ROY SHAW

Who's a pretty boy then?

This book contains stories of hard men, nutcases, chancers, psychos and troubled souls who have perpetrated unfathomable acts of wanton violence. Yet none come anywhere near matching bare-knuckle boxer Roy 'Pretty Boy' Shaw for the magnitude of the danger they pose to those who try to bar their path, or for the untrammelled ferocity of their temper. In the relentlessly hard world of illicit fighting, the Eastender was as fearless and uncompromising as they come, even proving a match for the infamous Lenny 'The Guv'nor' McLean.

The irony is that Shaw could have been a genuine contender had his life taken a different path. When AWOL from the army as an anti-authoritarian young man after being placed in the glasshouse and then the nuthouse, he fought ten bouts for Mickey Duff under the name 'Roy West', winning all of them, six by KOs. Duff, one of the grand old men of British boxing, rated Shaw a real talent but immediately dropped him when he found out he was on the run. Later in life, Shaw fought as a beefed-up middleweight and beat American Ron Stander, a talented heavyweight who had fought Joe Frazier and knocked out Ernie Shavers.

A career criminal who was in and out of prison, in 1963 he was sentenced to fifteen years for his part in an armed robbery in Dartford which was the biggest heist in Britain until the Great Train Robbery. Once inside, the prison services' most rebellious and ultra-violent inmate quickly began to make enemies and alienate warders, getting himself officially branded the most dangerous man in the whole British penal system as he killed a man in prison with his bare hands, slashed the throat of a former friend-turned-grass and shattered the jawbone of the governor of Broadmoor.

This one-man wrecking crew did time in twenty-one prisons, but his spell in the country's most notorious mental hospital following a diagnosis of insanity marked his most difficult period. The boxer was so consistently violent that he was eventually moved into the most feared place in the penal system: Broadmoor's dungeons. 'It was pitch black down there and the only sound was of lunatics wailing twenty-four hours a day,' wrote Shaw in his autobiography. 'I was beaten, experimented on, given drugs and even given electric shocks to the brain. But they never broke me, never had me where they wanted me.'

Weightlifting helped pass the time, especially in Parkhurst where he and Reggie Kray made the prison's three-man team the best in Britain. By the time he was released in 1973, he had changed shape completely, his 5ft 10in frame now a 16-stone ball of rock-hard muscle. But he remained a man for whom violence was second-nature: one of his first acts on getting out was to drop his estranged wife Carolina's new beau off a balcony, almost killing him. 'I like violence,' he said, 'it has been my friend and companion all my life.'

Shaw had been a regular at the boxing booths as a teenager, but got into bare-knuckle fighting by chance after he won £6,000 monstering gypsies at Barnet Fair. Word of his all-action style soon spread and within months he was fighting Donny 'The Bull' Adams, the self-styled King of the Gypsies, under Billy Smart's circus big top in Windsor in the biggest bare-knuckle fight ever staged. It was billed as a brutal encounter to be fought 'to the death', but Shaw's first, sledgehammer punch floored Adams before he stamped repeatedly on the regal pikey's head to ensure the encounter was at an end.

But it wasn't his encounters with Adams, his spell in Broadmoor, scary underworld connections or even his stoically psychopathic behaviour which defined Shaw: it was his three bouts with the monstrous Lenny McLean. Twelve years his junior, six inches taller than him and four stones heavier, McLean boasted that he was the veteran of 3,000 street-fights. The future star of cult gangster movie *Lock, Stock and Two Smoking Barrels* was certainly a feared enforcer, yet Shaw took him in the first of their three fights before losing two bloody battles in the underworld scene's equivalent of Leonard–Duran.

Now in his seventies, he was recently at a charity night in Perth for former world champion Ken Buchanan when a journalist asked how he deals with his anger now that he has retired. Shaw, who was sipping brandy from a crystal goblet, said nothing. Instead he just bit a large lump out of his glass which he then crunched, sending shards in all directions. The maddest, hardest septuagenarian of them all.

KEVIN WINN

Walter Mitty wants your body . . .

The moment when it all fell apart for Kevin Winn was the day when he appeared on television. Actually, it wasn't exactly Winn who was putting in a guest appearance on the small screen, but Scott Bradley, a player with the Seattle Mariners baseball team – the man he was impersonating. At that time, Winn, a balding, pudgy 25-year-old, was in bed, enjoying a cosy post-coital moment with his latest squeeze, one of the many women ('the number was well up into triple figures' he said) who were so desperate to bed even the most obscure pro sportsman that they'd allowed themselves to believe this unprepossessing specimen was a *top* sportsman. That's the point at which he'd empty their bank accounts and 'borrow' their cars.

No scout would have looked twice at him, but before he was sentenced to eighteen months in prison for fraud in 1992, the sports nut had managed to convince students, lawyers, military policewomen, secret service officers, hotel workers and nurses that he was any one of a collection of journeymen ice hockey or baseball players (both wear helmets, making identification difficult). At one stage he was dating a single mother *and* her two college-student babysitters. At another, his lie that he was Calgary Flames right wing Joey Mullen saw him end up giving an impassioned, tub-thumping speech as he addressed a sales convention of 1,000 delegates on the subject of 'being a winner'.

He even moved in with the parents of one new student girlfriend and spent more than a week playing golf and downing expensive wines with her tax lawyer father at his country club. Winn was Toronto Maple Leafs veteran Peter Zezel that week, which was unfortunate for him: one morning he came down to breakfast to be informed that he'd just been traded. Winn made his excuses and fled, taking daddy's Princeton ring and Pierre Cardin suit-cases as a momento.

A born charmer, the 5ft 7in 12-stone non-entity would persuade women – hundreds of attractive women – that his luggage and wallet had been misplaced by his airline. Then he'd milk them for food, boardings, and sex. Then he'd steal from them. Yet eventually American sport's most notorious Walter Mitty figure just conned too many women, took too many chances, stole too much money from too many girlfriends. But for a no-mark with no talent and no sporting pedigree, the three unforgettable years he spent impersonating America's C-list sports stars were golden. Even after being sentenced, he wasn't what anyone could describe as truly penitent.

'Whenever I could I'd let other people introduce me.

That gave me instant credibility,' he told *GQ*'s John Marchese. 'When women found out I was a professional athlete they usually wanted to go to bed with me right away. The way I figure it, it's to impress their girlfriends. Who wants to say "I went home with Joe who works at the bank" when they can say "I went home with a hockey player?"'

MATTI NYKANEN

Hell's angel

Thanks partly to a climate which can restrict daylight to just three hours a day, Finland has the highest incidence of suicides in the world and the lowest tolerance of alcohol. It is an extreme combination which makes for a high proportion of psychologically warped eccentrics and nutcases, and few are more damaged than ski jumping legend Matti Nykanen. The name of his autobiography – *Greetings from Hell* – pretty much sums him up.

The stick-thin, beak-nosed jumper has always been something of a character, a rake and a rascal who mixed childish charm with a godly talent for the sport which Finns revere above all others, with the possible exception of the javelin. While he was training and competing, winning three Olympic gold medals at Calgary in 1988 with a near-perfect performance, his appetite for partying was startlingly intense. The anorexic athlete would go on massive drinking binges and then sober up just in time to jump. But if he was near demented as a competitor, when he retired his behaviour became almost animalistic.

Like many athletes, Nykanen – who was almost six-feet tall but weighed under nine stone – struggled to find a role after he gave up ski jumping, although it wasn't for want of trying. First he tried running pizzerias, then he did some PR work and eventually he sold all of his Olympic and World Championship medals. He even dabbled in the music business, pressing a record that went gold in Finland, where it sold 25,000 copies. He eventually found his niche, though, as an exotic dancer at The Casino Club, a pole-dancing strip joint in a dormitory town just outside Helsinki.

But if Nykanen's methods of putting drink on the table varied, his *modus operandi* – crazy partying, drunken brawls, nights in cells and regular divorces – never varied. The other constant was the insatiable interest of the Finnish public in the bizarre workings of his public life and his regular scrapes with the law.

While he was still competing, Nykanen was seen as mildly insane but essentially lovable and irrepressible, but after he retired from ski jumping attitudes began to change, especially after 2004 when he went over to the dark side as his drinking spiralled out of control. The first body-blow occurred in March 2004 when he was fined £400 and received a four-year suspended sentence after he was found guilty of attacking his wife Mervi – with whom he regularly brawled in public – with a knife in Salzburg the previous year while under the influence.

If that was bad, worse was to come. In October 2004, the man who remains arguably Finland's greatest living athlete was sentenced to twenty-six months in chokey after he stabbed 60-year-old handyman Aarno Hujanen, who had been working on his country cottage. Nykanen, who 'really could not remember anything' about the incident, stabbed Hujanen twice in the back with a six-inch knife, severing an artery and almost killing the poor old fella. And what was the cause of an admittedly drunken argument that ruined one life and almost cost another? It apparently happened because Hujanen beat Nykanen in a finger-wrestling competition.

RODNEY O'DONNELL

Bad luck of the Irish

Irish rugby player Rodney O'Donnell was without a doubt the most superstitious man ever to play rugby, and quite possibly the most superstitious man in the history of organized sport. A player of great genius, his international career ended at the tender age of just 23 while playing for the Lions in South Africa when he tried to tackle legendary Springbok centre Danie Gerber during a game against Griqualand West. The rampaging Gerber, needless to say, was wearing the number thirteen. The injury that finished O'Donnell's career was two ruptured vertebrae – the sixth and the seventh.

O'Donnell was obsessed with the number thirteen. When it was the 13th day of the month he simply refused to come out of his hotel room; on tour in South Africa he steadfastly refused to enter any room whose digits could be combined to add up to thirteen. In fact, he even baulked at staying next door to such a room.

Not that thirteen was the only number which made Rodney's hair stand on end. Seven was another of his unlucky numbers, which explains why he wore extremely tight-fitting 32-inch shorts (his real size, 34, added up to seven). O'Donnell still blames Lions coach Noel Murphy for ending his career by insisting he wore a pair of size 34 shorts against Gerber's Griquas rather than his dirty, torn size 32s.

There was, almost literally, no end to O'Donnell's bizarre superstitions. One was his complete unwillingness to walk on any lines – whether they were between paving stones on the pavement or even those painted on the pitch. Room-mate John Beattie remembers going out for a meal with O'Donnell: 'If you were walking beside him and he stepped on a crack in the pavement, he would end up hundreds of yards behind you as he retraced his steps,' remembered the Scot. On one Friday 13th, fellow Irish Lions John Robbie and Ollie Campbell forced him to stay in his hotel room all day by taping lines all over the carpet outside his door.

O'Donnell would drive Noel Murphy mad by his refusal to go onto the team bus unless he was allowed to go on last, and by his refusal to go out for a game unless he was allowed to be the last man out of the dressing-room. Unfortunately, the last-man-out-of-the-dressing-room obsession was a superstition shared by Irish wildman Willie Duggan, with the result that one match in South Africa kicked off ten minutes late while both players tried to be the last one out onto the pitch. Duggan eventually gave in when he realized that it was either play with fourteen men or let O'Donnell go last.

Not that it stopped there. Once on the pitch O'Donnell had a strange set of actions before the game could begin, which included throwing the ball backwards through his own posts in the earnest belief that this would create a force field capable of repelling opposition penalties and conversions. According to Beattie, however, that was nowhere near his most insane routine – that occurred each evening when it was time to turn in. O'Donnell had a set routine that involved putting the phone on the hook 'the right way round', fixing the curtains in a particular pattern and making sure all the pictures were at a certain angle – all of which would take at least quarter of an hour. 'And then,' said Beattie, 'when he got into bed, he had to climb into it while touching the bottom sheet and the top sheet at exactly the same time. He would jump in until he got it right, which would often take him twenty or twenty-five attempts before he managed it.'

MARC CECILLON

Murder most foul

'Chantal, Chantal, where are you? I need you!' the colossus in the cell would cry, over and over again. Each time the Gendarme on guard duty would reply, as gently as possible: 'She's not coming. You killed her'. That would be the cue for a retching sob, followed by the mumbled words 'but that's not possible. I love her. She means everything to me, I owe her everything.'

When Marc Cecillon walked into his best friend Christian Beguy's birthday barbeque in a small village outside Lyons in the summer of 2004, whipped out his Magnum and pumped five bullets into his wife's head and chest in front of sixty stunned onlookers, he became more than a sporting legend. He became a genuine rival to Russian-roulette-playing Armand Vaquerin for the title of the craziest man in French rugby.

Not that everyone agrees that Cecillon was genuinely crazy or even culpable. One particularly unreconstructed hombre in his village told reporters that 'it takes real guts to kill your wife', while most of the men in the rugby-mad region outside Lyons believed that he was a chronically shy man pushed over the edge by a failing marriage and the recent end of a rugby career which had given his life form and meaning.

'Marc was always being invited to parties because people looked good if they had him as a guest and they bragged if they had spent an afternoon drinking with him,' said close friend and former France captain Jean-Francois Tordo. 'He couldn't say no but he found it a burden to be in such demand. He was a man with no limits. He did everything with passion. In a way, I think there was love in what he did – in killing her, I mean. At least there wasn't evil. I think what happened was the result of an accumulation of years of unexpressed emotions. He needed affection, he needed his friends but, equally, he did not show his emotions. He was this giant iceberg and we only saw the tip of him. There was such pain under the surface.'

In a country where 400 women are murdered each year by their partner and where the 'crime passionelle' is still a defence against murder, most of the women in Cecillon's village begged to differ with the verdict of male public opinion. Some even muttered darkly of rumours that Cecillon had a mistress and a son born out of wedlock. 'He was a drunk. He drank, he screwed, and he always got away with it because he was Marc Cecillon,' said Tordo's wife Pascal. 'That's what twenty years of alcohol does to you – little by little it destroys you. Marc could not cope with his life. When you kill your wife, you are killing your life.'

What is not in dispute is what happened on Saturday, 7 August 2004, a week after Cecillon's 45th birthday. Most of the party-goers at the barbeque in the small village of Saint-Savin were members of the nearby rugby club at Point de Cheruy and proceedings had been in full swing since early evening. Cecillon had arrived shortly after his wife, but the two had not spoken all night, and by 10 p.m. the former France captain was five times over the legal limit of alcohol and had become a slurring, hammered, accident waiting to happen.

At 11 p.m. his concerned hostess, Christian's wife Babeth, tried to persuade him to eat something, a suggestion to which he took violent exception, slapping her so hard that she was left with a black eye. He was immediately thrown out but within half an hour the Beguys' teenage son Alexandre heard the sound of Cecillon's Harley as he roared back to the party.

The rest is a matter of record. Cecillon walked straight up to Chantal, pulled out the Taurus Brazil 357 Magnum that he had purchased in South Africa in 1992 – the year he was named captain of France – and executed his wife, an act he has always maintained he was too drunk to remember. As soon as Cecillon had fired the gun, Alexandre threw a huge concrete breeze block at his head, but it 'just bounced off, as if it had made no impression'. It took ten men to subdue him and when police arrived they found him still struggling, tied to a chair with electrical cord and asking for Chantal.

ARRACHION

They don't make 'em like that any more . . .

Like every generation before us, and no doubt every one to follow, we are convinced that our contemporary sportsmen and women are the baddest, meanest, maddest and hardest ever. But while many express undying devotion to the cause, few of today's highly-paid and pampered sports stars are prepared to actually die to prove it. It was very different back in the mists of time, though, in the days of Ancient Greece when the Olympics had an unbroken run of 1,000 years of existence.

'These competitors, you see how they strain when they train, how much they put into it, even to the very utmost preferring to die (than to lose) during the Games,' wrote Greek chronicler Dion Chyrsostomos of the cult of death that surrounded the original Olympic Games.

The Olympics had come about as a sort of temporary truce to stop the warring Hellenic states from raping, pillaging and killing each other. The idea was that the Games would live up to George Orwell's corny old line about sport being 'war minus the shooting', but in reality they weren't too far short of mortal combat, with so much pride at stake that the death rate remained high. Even the penalty for any non-virginal woman who tried to watch was death, and if a champion from the previous Games was so presumptuous as to want to compete again, he did so on the strict understanding that he would be put to be death if he failed to beat all-comers.

It says much for a lunatic called Arrachion that he was one of the most feted Olympians after a millennium of fierce competition. Not only was he a double winner at pankarist – an extremely dangerous all-in fighting style which merged boxing and wrestling and in which only biting and eye-gouging were prohibited – but he also etched himself into the bloody history of the early Olympics by making the ultimate sacrifice at his third Games in 564 BC.

Caught in a stranglehold from his opponent as he sought to become one of the rare band of three-times winners at an Olympiad, Arrachion finally managed to get a hold on his opponent's leg. Even as he began to lose consciousness, the phenomenal strongman from the Peloponnes mountains tightened his grip on the limb. Yet even though he eventually dislocated his opponent's ankle and crushed his big toe, forcing the pain-racked fighter to raise his hands as a sign of withdrawal and defeat, Arrachion, in the words of witness Philostratos, 'had breathed his last'. Despite being dead, he was still adjudged the winner because his opponent had acknowledged defeat.

If Arrachion was undoubtedly the craziest cult hero

of Greek sporting mythology, Eurydamas the Cyrenean deserves a special mention in dispatches. In 672 BC he fought the fearsome champion Diappos from Kroton, and despite having had several teeth removed by a strong punch from his opponent, he decided to swallow them rather than let Diappos gain any encouragement by the sight of his discomfort. Iron Mike, eat your heart out.

AMELIA BOLANIOS

Suicide is painful

Welsh rugby fan Geoffrey Huish may have merited inclusion in this list for cutting off his own testicles as a tribute to his country's Six Nations grand slam in 2005, but he was a mere upstart compared to Amelia Bolanios. Not only was the demented Salvadorean teenager so distraught when her football team conceded a goal that she felt she had no option but to shoot herself through the heart with her father's pistol, but in doing so she triggered a four-day armed conflict that left 6,000 dead and threatened to engulf the whole of Central America.

The year was 1969 and the tiny country of El Salvador was in a state of turmoil. Relations with its larger neighbour Honduras had always been fraught but now they'd hit rock bottom after the Honduran government had expelled more than quarter of a million Salvadorean peasant farmers who had been working in Honduras. They had been given a month to leave the country and return to their dirt-poor homeland.

With relations between the two countries venomous and both engaged in an arms race ahead of what many saw as inevitable conflict, the last thing the region needed was for the two countries to stage a knockout tie to qualify for the 1970 World Cup in Mexico. But that's exactly what happened when the two countries were drawn together.

The first match was scheduled for 8 June and was to be played in Honduras's national stadium in Tegucigalpa. The Salvadorean players arrived the previous day and holed up in their hotel, where they had been met by an angry crowd which proceeded to beat sheets of tin and empty barrels with sticks, sound horns, throw stones, play Honduran marching music and let off fireworks throughout the night. It was a miracle that El Salvador's exhausted players only lost 1–0 the next day.

Back in El Salvador, however, events were taking a turn for the worse. Unable to cope as Honduran striker Roberto Cardona scored the winning goal in the final minute, an emotional Bolanios took her own life. In the febrile atmosphere of the time, she was immediately adopted as a martyr and given an elaborate state burial.

The 200,000-strong cortege which followed her body included every member of the national football team, who had been spat upon and humiliated in Honduras. It also included the President of the Republic and his ministers, all of them walking behind the flag-draped coffin.

The scene was set for war. The next day, the Honduran players arrived in El Salvador for the second leg of the World Cup qualifier. That night the windows of their hotel were smashed and rotten carcases and fruit thrown in. The noise was incessant throughout the night. On the day of the match the Honduran players had to be marched to the national stadium of Flor Blanc by soldiers riding in armoured cars and carrying sub-machine-guns. At the match the Honduran national anthem was shouted down, the country's flag burnt, and a dirty dishcloth run up the flagpole in its place.

El Salvador won 3–0 but by now the game was a mere detail. The visiting fans made a run for the border as gangs of local thugs shouting Bolanios's name hunted them down. Some didn't make it, and hundreds more woke up in hospital. 'Jesus, we're lucky that we lost,' said the visibly shaken Honduran coach Mario Griffin. Hours later the border was sealed and the next day an El Salvadorean warplane bombed the city of Tegucigalpa. The next 100 hours left more than 6,000 dead, 14,000 injured and almost 100,000 homeless.

Eighteen-year-old Amelia Bolanios may not have been the cause, but she was the trigger.

JON DRUMMOND

Clown prince of sprinters

Although a gospel singer who did a mean karaoke act, American Jon Drummond was never hugely popular with his fellow sprinters, even by the standards that exist among the most self-obsessed, over-paid and narcissistic cadre of competitors in the athletics firmament. Yet that all changed in Paris at the 2003 World Championships when the 100-metre specialist was disqualified for what was an admittedly marginal false start during the controversial 'one strike and you're out' period. That's when his fellow competitors started to *really* loathe him.

Drummond, a bombastic sprinter who had expected to be challenging Maurice Greene and Dwain Chambers for the world title, absolutely lost the plot in France. First, having false-started the tearful sprinter gestured like a madman to the stands, where the vocal Parisian crowd immediately showed its support for him. Then, having got the punters onside, he simply lay down in his lane, hands behind his head, refusing to move despite increasingly desperate entreaties from officials. Eventually, he ended up floating in the steeplechase water trap. By the time proceedings finally got underway, the 34-year-old had managed to delay the start of the quarter-final heat by more than an hour.

'Jon has always been known as the clown of track and field and I think he lost that title and became the idiot,' said a clearly unimpressed Olympic 100m champion Donovan Bailey as Drummond's epic tantrum drew to a close. 'You expect an American to make a song and dance of everything,' laughed French heptathlete Eunice Barber, before archly noting that Jamaica's Asafa Powell, Armenia's Vahagn Javakhyan and Swaziland's Machave Maseko and Mohamad Tamim had also been disqualified from the sprint without so much as a squeak of complaint.

'My spirit is broken because it has always been my desire to provide entertainment for the fans,' said an unrepentant Drummond. 'I felt very strongly that I was disqualified from the race unfairly and I protested my disqualification, but it was never my intention to harm the sport in any way or to inconvenience my fellow competitors or the fans.' Er, right you are, Jon.

The only other similar scene in major athletics history also occurred in the men's 100m, when Linford Christie refused to leave the track after being disqualified for a false start in the 1996 Olympic semi-final. There have, of course, been numerous other instances of sit-down protests in other sports, most notably at the 1988 Seoul Olympics when boxing homeboy Byun Jong-Il Byun was so angry at losing his bantamweight semi-final that he sat in the ring and refused to leave for several hours after he'd been hammered senseless by Bulgarian Alexander Hristov and had responded with a series of head-butts. An apoplectic Byun staged a silent protest for more than an hour, only giving up when organizers turned off the hall lights.

VLADIMIR TUMAEV

Football's Peter Panski

Can you imagine what sort of reaction there would be if Roman Abramovich or Malcolm Glazer played the last ten minutes of every game for the club they own? Or what commentators would say if Ron Noades or Doug Ellis substituted a player so that they could come on and take a penalty every time their side was lucky enough to be awarded one?

That, though, is exactly the scenario which has faced the fans of one of Siberia's biggest teams, Gazovik Gazprom, thanks to the Peter Pan syndrome of barmy chairman/owner/centre forward Vladimir Tumaev. The gas magnate, who is one of Russia's richest oligarchs through his ownership of Spetzgas Avtotrans, is a football obsessive who coulda-bin-a-contenda but instead dedicated his early years to the pursuit of gas rather than goals. But rather than let it drop, by 1988 the 41-year-old Siberian had amassed enough cash to indulge his dream of starting up a hometown team and, by 1995, when Gaz-Gaz had worked their way through regional leagues and gained promotion to the professional divisions, he also happened to have the time and inclination to do more than just wave from the directors box.

So, against the advice of the then head coach Vitaly Shevchenko ('Tumaev's only problem is what he wants and what is possible don't always match up,' was his pithy summary, which unsurprisingly doubled as his resignation) Vlad quickly became a regular fixture on the reserve bench. Coming on for the last ten minutes of each game, it took him less than four seasons to play his first 100 games for the club (and despite his 'help' they still managed to get promoted twice during that time). In 2003 he became the oldest man ever to score in a top-level game when he netted aged 56.

British fans would undoubtedly give the gaffer a hard time if he got ideas above his station in such a fashion, but in the middle of Siberia things work differently. Not only does Tumaev literally own half of the provincial city of Izhevsk, but he also directly or indirectly employs half of the town too. As the local MP he is a figure of authority, and as a karate black belt, expert marksman, top skier and self-proclaimed survival expert ('you could drop me anywhere in the forest with just a gun and I would survive') he is not a man to be messed with. Perhaps that's why he always got a standing ovation when he came out onto the pitch.

Not that applauding the boss is strictly necessary any more. Now 59, after 150 appearances and fifteen goals, Tumaev contents himself with playing for the veterans team. But he remains the same nutty eccentric who, when invited to Moscow to receive an award for services to football in 2002, flew his own helicopter onto the roof of the hotel where the ceremony was being held and then dispensed with the usual formalities and sung his favourite ballad to the great and the good of Russian football.

Tumaev's only real rival for nuttiest European football chairman – notwithstanding the strong claims of Messrs Gil, Berlusconi, Knighton, Hamman, Gaucci et al – is FC St Pauli's rampant self-publicist Cornelius Littmann. The gay dress-wearing German drag-artist is a former theatre owner and political comedian on Hamburg's famous redlight Reeperbahn, and as well as getting Günter Grass to perform spoken word shows at FC Pauli's run-down stadium to the club's supporters (described by *FourFourTwo* magazine as 'mainly punks, squatters and sex workers'), he was also notorious for an AIDS awareness campaign that featured a man giving a blowjob next to the slogan 'Take it out before you come'.

VERE ST LEGER GOOLD

Trunk call

Tennis is such a genteel pastime that few of its feistier exponents made it onto the long list for consideration for our Hall of Shame. One exception is Vere St Leger Goold, an aristocrat who ended the nineteenth century as a feted Wimbledon finalist and departed the twentieth century as a convicted and reviled murderer.

The younger son of a Baron from Waterford, Goold was a precociously talented young tennis player who won the prestigious Irish Open in 1879 without losing a set. What's more, his swashbuckling serve and volley style was a world removed from the dull baseline play of so many of his contemporaries, so that when later that summer the Irishman went to contest the Wimbledon Championship – only in its third year but already an important fixture of the Victorian social calendar – his arrival was eagerly awaited.

Contemporaries noted that Goold appeared to have been devastated to succumb meekly in straight sets in the all-comers final, where he was beaten by Reverend J.T. Hartley. The clergyman was certainly pretty surprised even to be playing judging by the fact that he was forced to shoot back to North Yorkshire on the Sunday rest day to deliver his weekly sermon. Whether it was the shock of that defeat or a bout of illness shortly afterwards, the Irishman failed to win a tournament of any note in the immediate aftermath and by 1883 had disappeared from the sporting scene altogether.

The next time Goold hit the headlines, it wasn't for his skill with a tennis racquet. Instead, he was plastered all over the front pages when in August 1907 he arrived at Marseilles on the train from Monte Carlo with his thrice-married French wife Marie and deposited a trunk and a handbag in the cloakroom, asking for them to be forwarded to London. The railway clerk, noticing an unpleasant smell coming from the trunk, fetched a police-man and had it prised open. Inside they found the chopped-up remains of a middle-aged woman.

The saga that unfolded captivated Edwardian Britain. The Goolds, it transpired, had married in 1891 and moved to Montreal but, having run out of funds, came back to Liverpool where they had squandered what remained of their money trying to set up a laundry business. Desperate for ready cash, they had gone to Monte Carlo to try their luck at the roulette wheel, but had quickly become reduced to penury by their losses in the casinos.

During the trial that followed the Goolds told a whole series of preposterous lies (first that they didn't know the dead woman, then that she was an acquaintance shot by a jealous boyfriend despite the absence of a gunshot wound) but could do little to stop the true story emerging. The victim was a Danish woman, Emma Liven, who had befriended the couple and lent them 1,000 francs and jewellery worth 80,000 francs. When she arrived at their home to demand repayment a heated row ensued and she was knifed countless times by Goold and his wife.

Vere tried to save Marie, but the prosecution successfully insisted that there were too many knife wounds, inflicted from too many angles, for the murder to be the work of one person. In 1908 both were found guilty of murder and received life sentences. They were to serve a total of just seven years though, with Marie dying six years later in Montpellier jail and Vere lasting little more than a year after being transported into appalling conditions on Devil's Island, the French penal colony off the coast of South America. He was just fifty-five.

Whether Goold was mad is open to question, but he was certainly bad and dangerous to know. Especially if you happened to be a wealthy Danish dowager.

JACKIE SHERRILL

A load of bullocks

When Jackie Sherrill was sacked as the coach of American football team Texas A&M in 1988 after taking them to the Cotton Bowl, he was determined not to get mad, but he would do just about anything to get even. In fact, make that *absolutely* anything.

Finally, after four years of waiting and stewing, the perfect chance to atone for his humiliation presented itself when his new charges, the little-fancied Mississippi State, were drawn to play Texas – the Aggies of College Station rather than the Longhorns of A&M, but still representatives of the Lone Star state – on the opening day of the 1992 collegiate season. No one gave Sherrill's men a chance of derailing the Aggies juggernaut. Desperate times, thought Sherrill, called for desperate measures.

The coach's raging desire to put one over on Texas's finest saw him adopt a bizarre motivational ploy. As the players went through their drills on the practice ground, he had a bull named 'Wild Willie' led onto the paddock and then made his bemused players gather round and watch as the poor beast was castrated in front of them.

'I should have done that on the South Farm, where they do it every day, instead of on the practice field,' said

Sherrill in reaction to the national outcry that followed as soon as news leaked out. 'But I'd still do it again. It was part-motivational and part-instructional; none of those poor boys even knew what a steer was, and that can't be right.'

Sherrill apologised unreservedly 'if this incident was in any way not perceived as proper by those who love Mississippi State'. He needn't have bothered: Mississippi State won the game 28–10 and no one was complaining. Except Wild Willie, of course.

Extreme motivational tactics are all very well, but in the increasingly politically correct world of American sport, are not necessarily sustainable even if they work. One man who found that to his cost was the enfant terrible of US college basketball, Bobby Knight.

Part-psychopath, part-genius, the chair-chucking head coach of Indiana University was known for having the shortest fuse in college sport during twenty-nine years at the helm. For three decades he was the most successful coach in college basketball, albeit one who was accused of motivational tactics that ranged from choking players to confronting students with a piece of used toilet paper. In 2000, after yet another physical altercation with a teenage student, the University called time on his all-too-controversial tenure.

CARL FAZIO JNR

Marketing madness

There is a point at which stupidity becomes madness. Carl Fazio Jnr, marketing man for the Cleveland Indians baseball team, didn't just cross that line when he decided that the best thing for flagging attendances and morale was a 10c beer night when the Texas Rangers visited the Indians' Municipal Stadium in June 1974, he blew it away. A free gun with every ticket sold might have been a worse idea, but it would still have been a close run thing.

For a start, there was the context. Relations between the two clubs had long been spiky. Just a week earlier, the Indians and Rangers players had fought at the Texans' Arlington Stadium after a confrontation between visiting pitcher Milt Wilcox and home batter Lenny Randle had sparked an all-out brawl. As the players slugged it out, Rangers fans barracked the Indians' players and soaked them with beer.

As the backdrop for a 10c beer offer, it didn't augur well, but at least the struggling baseball team's marketing genius got it half right. The Indians, mired in the bottom half of the AL East and with their worst crowd figures since the Second World War, experienced exactly the sort of upturn in attendance that they craved, with the number of bums on seats surging from an average of 8,000 the previous season to well over 25,000 on that balmy summer night.

If that's the good news, the downside was the state of the fans. Most were drunk before they arrived, and the ones that weren't were busy making up for lost time. And they all had one thing in common, which was a desire to exact some sort of revenge for the perceived slight from the week before. Even before the game had started, the assembled pressmen and club officials heard explosions coming from the stands.

As soon as the game started, the ferment in the stands began to spill over. Literally. First on was a large woman who displayed her prize assets for the benefit of the Rangers players; next up was a naked Indians fan who slid into second base in the middle of play; then came a father and son combo, who mooned rookie of the year Mike Hargrove. By this stage a constant succession of drunken Indians fans were finding their way into the outfield.

By the time the Indians came in to bat, a few tankerloads of beer had been consumed and the place was bedlam. Within minutes the bases were loaded and the home side would surely have drawn level had they got the chance. But they didn't. All of a sudden a hail of batteries, rocks, bottles, and golf balls rained down upon the Rangers' star outfielder Jeff Boroughs, who was running towards the main stand in hot pursuit of a fan who had stolen his glove. Suddenly Boroughs found himself isolated and surrounded by hostile fans.

Rangers coach Billy Martin, himself a legendary hell-raising scrapper, saw what was happening. Grabbing a bat and dodging through the flying chairs and rocks, he led the visiting bench and several Indians players into the outfield to retrieve Boroughs. The hand-to-hand combat was frightening: it was Iwo Jima without the flame-throwers. 'The bat showed up later and it was broken,' said Hargrove.

As the rescue mission continued in the outfield, umpire Nestor Chylak was clattered by a rock and a chair, and quickly forfeited the game to the Rangers. 'They were just uncontrollable beasts,' Chylak told baseballlibrary.com when asked about the Indians supporters. 'I've never seen anything like it, except in a zoo.'

For all that the riot shook Cleveland to its foundations, the most amazing aspect of the whole fiasco wasn't the fact that the riot police had to be called, nor even the fact that there were only nine arrests and no bodybags. It was the fact that demented marketing genius Fazio Jnr was still determined to carry on with the remaining 10c beer nights until he was forcibly warned off by AL president Lee MacPhail with the inimitable words: 'There was no question that beer played a great part in this affair.'

GENNADIY TUMILOVICH

Showed real bottle

In his native Belarus, they suspected that talented young Dinamo Tbilisi keeper Gennadiy Tumilovich was going to rack and ruin in 1991 when he had his first scrape with authority aged just 17. After an epic vodka-downing marathon he ended up stealing the team bus which, true to later form, he crashed.

Immediately arrested by the local constabulary, he was in the process of having a good old-fashioned kicking administered by the police when one of them recognised what was left of him and ensured he was released.

Just in case anyone was in any doubt that his relationship with vodka was one that would cause problems throughout his career, his next stunt was to miss training after an all-night bender, following which he turned up at his club wearing a plaster-cast in an attempt to garner the sympathy vote (he failed).

His next high-profile wheeze occurred during the vital final negotiations for his lucrative move to Russian side Chernomorets Novorossiisk. Bored with waiting for the details to be ironed out, Tumilovich decided to kill some time in the usual manner. A bottle of vodka later, and the last his prospective owners heard of him was the screeching of tyres as he left Dinamo's training ground at top speed, a manoeuvre which was quickly followed by a complete loss of control and the high-velocity meeting of his car with a lamp-post. At least that collision slowed his progress just enough to stop his front wheels right on the edge of a precipice.

Much-travelled in the Nineties ('he didn't suit us as a player, and he didn't suit us as a man,' said Rostselmash club owner Anatoly Baidachny on sacking him, a sentiment with which most of his former clubs agreed), he has not touched a drop of booze since he started a course of hypnosis in 1998. Although being sober has helped him hold down a job and saw him named Belarus's player of the year in 2001, Tumilovich isn't convinced that it's actually made him a better player. 'As soon as I stopped drinking my game just fell apart,' he said, 'but at least I feel great now. No more hangovers.'

JUAN MARICHAL

Assault and battery

For wanton violence on camera, nothing can beat an incident which occurred in August 1965 during a game between two of baseball's fiercest rivals, the San Francisco Giants and the LA Dodgers.

There was a long history of bad blood between the two behemoths of American baseball, and that summer it was threatening to spill over again throughout a bad-tempered match at the Giants' Candlestick Park. The spark for the explosion that was to come on 22 August occurred two days earlier when Dodgers catcher Johnny Roseboro was accused of trying to 'bean' (throw the ball so that it hits an opponent on the head) the Giants' Matty Alou.

One player who took particular exception to the incident was the Giants stylish Latino pitcher, Juan Marichal. Alou's best friend, 'The Dominican Dandy' took it upon himself to gain revenge by launching potentially lethal beanballs at the heads of two Dodgers batsmen. Although neither was injured, when it came to Marichal's turn to bat, Dodgers catcher Roseboro wanted him to get a taste of his own medicine and loudly encouraged pitcher Sandy Koufax to 'get into' the Dominican.

In the circumstances, there could only be one outcome, and sure enough the two men were soon involved in a fierce verbal confrontation. Which is when Roseboro made what was almost a fatal error – he took off his mask to remonstrate further with Marichal. And then it happened. In front of a live television audience and 50,000 witnesses, Marichal repeatedly smacked Roseboro over the head with his baseball bat in the most savage attack ever witnessed on television. Only the mass intervention of all the players from both sides, leading to one of the great scraps of all time, saved Roseboro. After being led away concussed and covered in blood, he spent the rest of the afternoon having his head stitched up.

Despite widespread revulsion, Marichal was only fined $1,750 and banned for a week.

Just to prove that the North American influence has a way of corrupting otherwise sane foreign nationals, the normally laid-back Pakistani cricketer Inzamam ul-Haq was involved in a similar batsman-swats-annoying-fella scenario while contesting the Sahara Cup against India in Toronto in 1997.

Inzamam, a veteran of ten years of Test cricket, had finally cracked after two days of abuse directed at him from the stands by megaphone-wielding Indian barracker Shivkumar Thind. Having endured taunts in Hindi about his size and his family background, Inzamam broke ranks and charged into the grandstand to sort out Thind after the Indian fan called him a 'fat potato'. Although police moved in quickly to make arrests, they were unable to prevent a major scuffle breaking out between the cricket bat-wielding Inzamam and Thind, who launched his megaphone at the rampaging batsman before engaging him in hand-to-hand combat.

Later charged with assault with a deadly weapon, perhaps Inzamam would have been better advised to follow the example of West Indian bowler Sylvester Clarke. On tour in Pakistan in 1981, Clarke was first verbally abused by the spectators in Multan and then, when he showed no signs of rising to the bait, was showered with orange peel. Cool as can be, Clarke simply bent down, picked up one of the bricks used to mark the boundary and hurled it into the crowd, knocking out the main troublemaker.

EMPEROR TRAJAN

Imperial leatherer

If you're talking about hard-core sporting madness, nothing on earth has ever come close to matching the lunacy of the Romans, a society with a fanatic interest in games which were genuinely extreme. At the Circus Maximus, where a crowd of 250,000 would watch up to thirty chariot races each day, the body count was steady but unspectacular. But a couple of miles down the road at the Colosseum, the bloodlust and death toll occurred on an altogether more epic scale.

In a landscape populated by a mixture of the genuinely insane and those fighting for their lives, a couple of ancient headcases stand out. The Emperor Commodus (memorably played by Joaquin Phoenix in the film *Gladiator*) was so in thrall to the arena that he used to disguise himself as a gladiator and go out to fight the criminals, heretics, slaves and assorted psychopaths who made up the vast bulk of the gladiatorial caste. He also paid himself a million sesterces from the public purse for each such performance, an amount so vast that he eventually came close to bankrupting the Roman Empire.

Commodus was undoubtedly a bit nutty (he demanded to be worshipped as a god, slept with his sister and had a harem of 300 men and women), yet the most barbaric behaviour often came from those Emperors who remained in the stand. Emperor Titus, for example, had 5,000 wild animals and 4,000 domestic animals killed during the 100-Day Show to celebrate the opening of the Colosseum. In AD 249, Emperor Philip celebrated the one thousandth anniversary of the founding of Rome by throwing a bash at the Colosseum during which the following were slaughtered: 1,000 pairs of gladiators, thirty-two elephants, ten tigers, sixty lions, thirty leopards, ten hyenas, ten giraffes, twenty asses, forty horses, ten zebras, six hippos, and one rhino.

Yet for all that Commodus, Titus, and Phil were renowned gore-merchants, none came close to matching the excesses of the Emperor Trajan. He wanted to mark his military triumph in Dacia (modern day Romania) in unforgettable style and dreamed up a 122-day Festival at the Colosseum, an event which must remain the bloodiest 'sporting' spectacle of all time. What's more, contemporary chroniclers record that the otherwise measured and sane Trajan was in attendance every day and that he gloried in the gore.

During four months of bloodshed, 11,000 Jews, Christians, slaves and gladiators – plus more than 10,000 animals – were literally put to the sword. So severe was the pressure put upon stocks of some wild animals that Trajan is reckoned to be directly responsible for the extinction of the European lion, the aurochs, the Libyan elephant and possibly the African bear. Not only that, but animals such as the hippo and rhino were wiped out in areas such as North Africa.

JIM BROWN

When Gandhi met Rambo

On the face of it, Jim Brown is one of the most admirable figures ever to have graced America's fields of dreams. Born in the Thirties during the Jim Crow era, he was a driven kid who raised himself from an impoverished, segregated black community in Georgia to attend an all-white private school on Long Island before putting himself through university and going on to become the greatest running back ever to play American Football. 'For mercurial speed, airy nimbleness, and explosive violence in one package of undistilled evil, there is no other like Mr Brown,' wrote Pulitzer Prize winning sports columnist Red Smith.

Then, aged just 30, the Cleveland Browns legend gave it up to star in the film *The Dirty Dozen* and to campaign for improved race relations, as he had to his own detriment throughout his NFL career. At the same time, he preached the gospel of non-violence and used his kudos with disenfranchised inner-city black kids to try to stem the rising tide of gang-related violence. Spike Lee, who produced an hour-long biopic of Brown's life, compared him to Gandhi. Brown compared himself to Nelson Mandela.

All well and good, but there's some bad stuff too. Lots of it, in fact. For a start, several times Brown has been charged with beating up women.

His first highly-publicised brush with the law came in 1965, when an 18-year-old accused Brown of plying her with whisky before forcing her to have sex with him. After a ten-day trial, the star-struck jury found him not guilty of assault and battery after they accepted his argument that sex had been consensual.

The twelve good men and true who acquitted Brown might not have been so keen to accept his version of events had they been in possession of a crystal ball. Three years later in 1968, Brown was charged with intent to murder after 22-year-old French model Eva Marie Bohn-Chin fell from a second-storey balcony during a fracas with him. This time it never went to trial as a terrified Bohn-Chin refused to name Brown as her assailant.

There were violent outbursts against men as well – in

1969 he was acquitted of assaulting a man after a traffic accident and in 1978 he was fined and served a day in jail for beating up his golf partner – but most of his aggression was directed towards girlfriends or women who he wanted to become girlfriends.

In 1972 he was charged with battering two women, but the charges were dropped after both refused to testify. In 1985, he was charged with rape, sexual battery and assault against a 33-year-old woman, but once again the charges were dropped. The next year, charges resulting from a beating he allegedly handed out to his 21-year-old fiancée – she was flirting apparently – were dropped after he had spent just three hours in jail. His fiancée refused to help the police with their enquiries.

Brown eventually ended up in the slammer in 1999 when his petrified wife, Monique, rang 911 and said he was threatening to snap her neck. She later detailed a long history of beatings, black eyes, choking incidents, and of a threat to impale her on a metal spear before recanting during the trial, saying that she had lied to get attention and that she had provoked the confrontation by accusing Brown of being unfaithful. Prosecutors had to settle for convicting him of vandalism for smashing the window of Monique's car with a shovel.

Even then, he would have got off with a fine and probation, but he refused to attend domestic violence counselling or do either forty hours of clean-up or 400 hours of community service. Telling the judge that 'I ain't gonna pick up no paper for nobody', he did four months in the slammer instead.

At least that gave him time to reflect on the error of his ways and by the time he got out of the big house, Brown finally knew where the blame for his errant behaviour lay. He had initially blamed a white conspiracy for his conviction but now knew, he said, that his anger towards his wife and women in general was cause by the female menstrual cycle. 'I have struggled with their PMS,' he admitted.

Few women seem to have had a good word to say about Brown. He made his name as an actor with a steamy love scene with Raquel Welch in *100 Rifles*, which established him as the testosterone-laden epitome of macho virility, but Welch was far from impressed. 'The ideal candidate for an actor needs that little bit of femininity,' she ventured, 'and Jim, as far as I can see, has not got an ounce of femininity in him.'

Perhaps the saddest indictment of all came from Brown's two children. 'I wanted to be daddy's little girl and he wasn't there,' said daughter Kim. His son Kevin, now in his forties, says his father has hugged him just once in his life.

TARIBO WEST

Devon-sent

God-bothering Nigerian defender Taribo West – yep, the one famous for wearing fetchingly feminine lime green braids in his hair at the 2002 World Cup – is no David Icke, but he's hardly your run-of-the-mill superstar footballer either. In fact, given his recent assertion that 'the voice of God was telling me to go [to Plymouth Argyle]' you have to wonder whether, in the process of finding the good Lord, he misplaced all sense of reason.

West may be a man of God these days, but in his youth he flirted with an early meeting with his maker. After moving to Lagos from sleepy Port Harcourt as a teenager, he fell in with a gang called the Area Boys and took to a life of break-ins, fighting, drugs and violent muggings. Only when his best friend was stabbed to death in front of him did he hightail it back to Harcourt to concentrate on his footballing studies.

Reformed and refocused, in 1993 he joined French side Auxerre, moving four years later to his boyhood heroes, Inter Milan. However, the defender had barely begun to savour la dolce vita when things took a decidedly religious twist with the arrival of his evangelically turbo-charged

sister Patient, who was at the time living and preaching in the States.

His sister may be many things but patient is not one of them. As soon as West opened the door to his flat, she said 'you must be strong to live in a house like this. It has a bad aura. What kind of rituals have you been performing?'

She wasn't, as it turns out, too far off the mark. 'I was very superstitious and before every game I would light a candle and hold a magical stone that a friend had brought me back from Israel,' said West. 'My sister said she could feel occult energies and she said she could see two dogs – one white and one black – fighting it out in my house.'

Despite the presence of malevolent spirits, Patient grabbed forty winks while Taribo was at training. When he returned she confronted him with news of her vivid dream of purity. 'I realised then that I needed God's help,' said West. 'So we knelt down and prayed. As we did so, all the drawers in the house began to open and shut. I thought it might be just the wind, but as that thought entered my head, all the doors began to bang as well. It was like something from a bad film, but I knew it was reality. I experienced a warm feeling inside, and then my sister turned to me and said: "Taribo, you will be a pastor, too".'

Since that day, Pastor West has dedicated his spare time and wealth to ministering to the poor through his

Shelter in the Storm church in the Milanese suburb of Affori – 'creating the miraculous through the ludicrous' as fellow pastor Ayo Don-Dawodu said of him. Even when he was fined £20,000 and shipped out to Kaiserslautern after a dressing-room ruck with Inter coach Mircea Lucescu, he still came back to preach in Milan each week, which wasn't universally welcomed when it caused him to miss an away game at St Pauli. That's when the Bundesliga club sacked him.

West has allowed himself to be guided by God ever since, and the Almighty has taken him to some mighty strange destinations. Like Derby. And Middlesbrough. 'Before I went to Qatar I had a revelation,' said the defender. 'I saw myself playing in a stadium in front of a small crowd. I saw myself playing in a certain type of shirt and with a certain group of people. When I arrived at the club to discuss joining them it was the same stadium I had seen in my revelation. They were playing in the same shirt. I just knew it was right.

'Three or four days before I came to Plymouth I had a similar experience. I saw myself playing for a Second Division team in Spain. At first that made me think that Plymouth weren't right for me. Besides, my human nature was telling me that I should be playing for a top division team somewhere. I woke up and I was thinking to myself: "I don't want to play for a Second Division team". Then I realised that God was simply showing me a sign that I would join a Second Division team somewhere. It was the voice of God. The spirit was telling me: "Taribo, you have to go to Plymouth". And I went because I could have been an arrogant football star who lived life through rose-tinted glasses, but God saved me from that.'

MITCH 'BLOOD' GREEN

Streetfighter

A 6ft 5in. bombastic colossus of ripped muscle and menacing intent, Mitch 'Blood' Green was a Golden Gloves winner who ended his professional career with a record of 18–6–1. He'd administered eleven sledgehammer KOs and he'd fought the best in the world. No one had ever knocked him down, no one ever beat him bloody.

Yet if Green's name is mentioned, none of that counts. All that anyone remembers is one cold morning in Harlem in 1988 when Green and Mike Tyson came to blows at 5 am outside Dapper Dan's, New York's super-bling clothing emporium. It was a fleeting and one-sided encounter completely provoked by Green. Wailing gibberish and cursing like a madman, he made it past Tyson's enormous entourage and even managed to unleash a couple of haymakers at the champion of the world, but

Tyson's quick-fire two-fisted response, delivered via knuckles wrapped in lacerating gold, left Green lying in a corner with a broken nose and a deep gash that required five stitches.

'Hey man, I always did a lot of my fighting in the street anyway,' said Green, who was a gang leader ruling swathes of New York while Tyson, the juvenile delinquent, was still relieving little old ladies of their handbags. 'I like to fight. I'm dedicated to it. That's why my name is Mitch 'Blood' Green, you know. If I didn't make 'em bleed, I wasn't satisfied. If I didn't scratch 'em or bloody their nose, I wasn't satisfied. I got the name when I was 14 or 15. And it's stuck for a reason.'

That impromptu rematch with Tyson wasn't the end of the matter though. Tyson had beaten Green on points over ten rounds two years before, but the result was overshadowed by the locker-room barney that broke out when the challenger found out shortly before the fight that instead of the usual 3–1 split, he was earning $30,000 compared to Tyson's cool million. That's when he went mad and fought promoter Don King's whole troop of bodyguards before finally going out and losing to Iron Mike. ('If I'd been paid right, I'd have knocked the faggot out,' he later claimed with absolutely no justification). The street-scrapping was his first attempt to get payback. His second was the subsequent court appearance.

Despite the fact that it had been Green who had stalked Tyson and initiated the Harlem brawl, he sued Tyson for assault, claiming damages of $25m. During what must surely have been the most bizarre court proceedings until O.J. Simpson ambled into view, Green constantly barracked Tyson as a 'homo' in the courtroom, refusing to refer to the accused as anything other than 'Michelle Tyson'. Despite Tyson's lisping protestations that he was the victim, Green got $45,000, not even enough to cover his legal bills.

'I still beat him in court,' crowed Green. 'All he did was sit there and say in his sissy voice, "He hit me first! He hit me first!" I called him a homo on national TV, and he did nothing. I'd bust him up good if I had the chance now.'

At least Tyson can defend himself. The other object of Green's enduring ire, promoter Don King, is absolutely terrified of the boxer, which is hardly surprising given that Green broke into his office, chucked the contents out of the 23rd floor window and then dangled King out of the same window by his ankles. 'Everything in boxing is about getting a purse that you can retire on,' reasoned Green, 'but Don King, Don Queen, denied me, sold me out. I hate Don King, man. I hope he chokes on a chicken bone. He's a devil; his hair hides his horns.'

If all of that leaves the impression that Green is infamous for one event, that would be to underestimate one

of boxing's nuttiest alumni. Now a nightclub bouncer, he
is a magnet for every punk who fancies himself ('I call
myself 'The Bouncing Boxer' 'cos I don't mind getting
into a little brawl. I still want to fight. I can fight. I can
knock anyone out'), but nor is he averse to going out
and finding trouble himself. Shortly before his ruck with
Tyson, too much PCP sent him on a window-smashing
rampage through Harlem that took half a dozen of New
York's finest to bring to a halt.

Green also holds what must be a record for traffic
violations. At the last count, he had just broken into triple
figures, including one arrest for driving with a portable
TV set mounted on his dashboard. Possibly his maddest
moment, though, was when he robbed a petrol station
and then – instead of scarpering – proceeded to fill up the
tanks of waiting motorists before pocketing their pay-
ments, leading inevitably to yet another stint in the
slammer.

ALBERT BELLE

For whom the Belle tolls

Volatile, violent and utterly lacking in grace or redeeming features, Albert Belle was almost certainly the least popular baseball player of the modern era. And that's some boast for a player who was a prodigiously gifted athlete in a nation where that usually excuses virtually any excesses or character flaws.

Despite stellar stats, both the fans and the media loathed him. Hell, even his peers despised him to the point where batting figures that should have guaranteed him entry to the Hall of Fame counted for nothing when it came to a secret ballot. Needing 390 votes to enter the Hall of Fame in 1995, Belle got just forty, losing out to popular but limited Boston first baseman Mo Vaughn, a player who would otherwise have stood little chance of joining the Cooperstown elite.

So why was Belle so widely disliked and despised? It's difficult to know where to start. Besides generally conversing with the media using only grunted profanities (he was once fined $50,000 for yelling obscenities at a reporter) the media also hated him because he once tried to beanball a pitchside photographer.

Not that it was the only time he used a baseball as a

weapon. In 1991, a drunken heckler made references to Belle's problems with alcohol and DUI convictions, taunting the player by shouting the hated nickname 'Joey' at him. Not one to take insults lying down, Belle threw a potentially lethal fastball into the offender's chest from less than fifteen feet, sending the heckler to hospital and earning Belle a fine and a one-week suspension.

Belle particularly likes beating up defenceless hecklers, women and children. Sometimes he got ambitious and did all three at once. In 1988, while playing for the White Sox, he chucked his bat into the stands, hitting a 10-year-old girl in the face and leaving her lying in a pool of blood. That was around the time that the American League forced him to undergo anger-management counselling after he chased a bunch of young trick-or-treaters in his truck before trying to run them over.

Women have fared even worse. He was arrested for punching one girlfriend and then smashing up her house, and he has two felony charges of stalking on his rap sheet. One terrified ex-girlfriend who was being threatened by Belle on a daily basis couldn't work out how he kept turning up at her gym, disrupting dates and generally ruining her life until, one day, a GPS tracking device fell off the underside of her car.

Okay, so that's the media, fans, women, and children accounted for. But what of his peers: why did they hate him quite so much? It could, of course, be the cheating (he was suspended for seven games in 1994 for corking his bat at Comiskey Park). It could be the violence (in 1994 he was suspended after instigating a brawl by elbowing an opposing player). Or what about the gambling on games (he was implicated in two investigations into gambling on sport and admitted to a $40,000 loss in a formal legal deposition)? Or maybe it's his habit of abusing fellow pros and respected back-room staff (belittled hitting instructor Von Joshua and berated old-school general manager Ron Schueler, to name but two). It might even be his habit of racking up easy stats in the matches that didn't matter, and going MIA in the matches that did. Or maybe it's just resentment that he pulled in almost £100m in salary during his twelve-year career by flitting from one high-paying team to another. Take your pick.

LEIGH RICHMOND ROOSE

Mad dogs and Welshmen

Even in the era of Edwardian football, gentleman goal-keeper Leigh Richmond Roose was something of a Corinthian anachronism. An eccentric who insisted on wearing white gloves and a twin-peaked cap, and who put on gymnastic displays along the crossbar to keep fans entertained, he was one of the most memorable amateurs ever to have played the game at the top level.

And make no mistake, despite being an amateur, Roose did play at the highest level. As well as representing Wales, Everton, Arsenal, Aston Villa, and Celtic among a host of clubs, he played for Sunderland ninety-two times over three seasons between 1907–1910, helping the Wearside club to finish second in the league on two occasions, and, according to the club's official history 'almost single-handedly' saving the team from relegation in his final season. Sir Frederick Wall, the then head of the FA, believed he was 'such a sensation as a goalkeeper [because he was such] a clever man who had the eccentricity of genius. His daring was seen in the goal, where he was often taking risks and emerging triumphant.'

Yet despite being a renowned penalty-saver and something of a phenomenon between the sticks, Roose will not be remembered for his prowess on the field but for his singular behaviour off it. An eminent bacteriologist, the Welshman showed scant concern for his personal hygiene and insisted on wearing the same 'lucky' shorts and undershirt (the latter was an old black-and-green Aberystwyth top) throughout his twelve-year career, neither of which he would allow to be washed. When Arsenal trainer George Hardy mistakenly sent them off to be laundered, Roose was so angry he had to be restrained from attacking him.

Like the empire-building muscular Christians of the nineteenth century, Roose the Welsh minister's son was not one for passing up the chance for a good barney. Once the 6ft 3in. bruiser assaulted a Sunderland director, beating him so badly that he was banned for fourteen days by the FA.

On the pitch, his play featured a virtually psychotic disregard for his own safety and a desire to rough up opposing centre forwards, a combination shared by his cousin, renowned Welsh rugby international Jack Jenkins. Roose's thuggish streak showed up at school in Holt in North Wales, where he kicked then schoolmaster H.G. Wells so hard in the kidneys that he was stretchered off the field and incapacitated for several weeks.

Playing in an era when most keepers rarely left their line, he would rush off his to confront opponents. 'Roose enjoyed taunting experienced international forwards, some of whom felt the full force of his fist in goalmouth mêlées,' wrote one biographer. He once sparked a riot when he and the equally celebrated Herbert Chapman guested for Port Vale reserves against his current club Stoke and Roose performed so magnificently that he denied Stoke the reserve team league championship. Only the intervention of the police saved him from being thrown in the river Trent by the raging 7,000-strong crowd who invaded the pitch. His first international match was also marked by the same approach as Roose rushed off his line to shoulder-charge an Irish winger on the distant touchline, knocking him out of play and leaving him unconscious.

The extravagantly extrovert Roose was nevertheless a born crowd-pleaser. During matches, he would sit and chat to fans, and in a *Daily Mail* readers poll before the First World War he was far and away the first choice as the best goalkeeper of all time. He also forced a change in the laws of the game. Before 1912, keepers were allowed to handle anywhere in their own half, and Roose loved being a part of the attacks so used to carry the ball to the halfway line.

A man of independent means, Roose cut a very glamorous figure in Edwardian society in his Savile Row or full morning suits. He squired numerous society beauties, including the famous music hall star Marie Lloyd, and in 1905 was voted the second most glamorous bachelor in Britain after Jack Hobbs. Although playing as an amateur, Roose charged clubs astronomical expenses. Once, when playing for Stoke at Aston Villa, he missed the London to Birmingham train so he simply hired a train and had the enormous £31 bill sent to the Potteries club.

Roose died as he had lived: at full throttle. As a famous 37-year-old socialite, he could have avoided service in 1914 had he wanted, but he insisted on volunteering as a private. However, after winning the military medal and promotion for his lunatic grenade-throwing sorties, he simply went missing in action at the Somme in 1916. His body was never found.

ALBERTO CARLOS MARTINEZ

Fangs ain't what they used to be

A lot of the stories here have taken time to tell. Some men have packed a lot of madness or badness into their lives, but the tale of well known Argentine television director Alberto Carlos Martinez – the larger-than-life man who actually first brought telly to the Pampas in the 1950s – doesn't take a long time to tell. About as long, in fact, as it took for the offence which gained him entry to *Notorious* took to commit.

It was in 1957 and the 25-year-old Martinez was a gifted young rugby player turning out for Obras Sanitarias in the first division of the Buenos Aires League against local rivals Municipalidad. As ever in Argentina, a country where the game is played with an unrivalled ferocity, it wasn't long before things started getting a bit feisty. Referee Oscar Aicardi, from the nearby Los Tilos club, was struggling to keep a lid on proceedings when all hell broke loose as a 30-man fight broke out on the halfway line.

When the dust had settled, it turned out that the cause of the ruckus was the decision of Municipalidad's fullback to take the law into his own hands and kick Martinez in the face, resulting in the loss of several teeth (not that the ever-sozzled hooker would necessarily have noticed the pain). Not one to take things lying down, Martinez had responded in kind, pinning the fullback down and biting a large chunk out of his stomach.

Alerted by the prone player's screams, referee Aicardi identified the injured man and diagnosed the injury (not that it was exactly difficult given the teeth marks and a bloody trail of evidence). Finding the culprit was altogether more difficult, but the presence of teeth marks made it easy: he simply took a look at the teeth of each of the Obras Sanitarias players.

Although Martinez had lost a lot of teeth, he was also the only player present with bloody fangs – and the only possible culprit. Sent before the beaks, he was banned for an unprecedented and entirely unreasonable ninety-nine years. Now 74, he is eligible for his rugby parole in 2056, at which stage he will be 124 years old.

KEN 'FLEX' WHEELER

Officer Steroids

Bodybuilding is replete with nutters, none more so than Ken 'Flex' Wheeler. During the Nineties, when Wheeler was in his pomp, virtually all of the top bodybuilders used enormous quantities of steroids, but few consumed more than the enormous man they nicknamed the Sultan of Symmetry. And none who lived were more successful at ravaging their bodies than Wheeler.

A small weedy kid born into abject single-parent poverty in Fresno, California, Wheeler had a troubled upbringing marked by bullying and sexual abuse in which he claims he was first abused as a five-year-old by two female teenage babysitters. Mired in an existence of petty crime and with a pregnant girlfriend, he staged his first suicide attempt at just 14 when he drove his moped in front of a truck on the motorway. When that failed he swallowed a whole bottle of asprin.

The troubled teenager's life changed forever when he was sent to live with his father. A school gridiron coach, his dad didn't have enough time to look after his boy and instead plonked him in the gym each day after school. It was a Eureka moment for the young martial artist. By the age of 18, when he first took steroids, his body was already ripped and honed. Within a year of going on the juice his weight had jumped from 140lbs to 200lbs, later going on to almost 300lbs.

Wheeler's appetite for steroids was insatiable. He would act as an experimental 'lab' for older gym rats, and took any drugs they offered, no matter how little was known about them. The veterans would laugh as he literally grew before their eyes, but steroids took a heavy toll. By the time Wheeler hung up his posing pouch, his body was so weakened by years of abuse, by his industrial intake of steroids and the diuretics that regularly left him doubled up in excruciating pain, that when the abuse was exacerbated by the premature onset of a disease known as FSGS his kidney simply packed in. Only the donation of a replacement organ by a member of his church – he had just become a born-again Christian – saved his life.

Aged 31, his body called time on his bodybuilding career. By then he was so 'whacked' that he missed one Mr Olympia contest because he'd been 'car-jacked by ninjas'. On another occasion, he hallucinated so badly that he believed his leg had turned into a dog and attacked it. His use of diuretics was severe and his body was so desperate for air that he'd faint every time he went on a rollercoaster.

Wheeler redefined what was needed to succeed. Asked about his life when he was in the midst of the manic year of 1997 in which he won the Ironman, Arnold Classic, and San Jose Classic, he replied simply that: 'I eat. I sleep. I train. Period.' Spending at least ten hours a day in the gym and ingesting huge quantities of steroids meant Wheeler was not a man you'd want to be around. 'You're super aggressive,' he said of the 'roid rage which had got him nicknamed 'Officer Steroids' for beating up tramps and drunks when he worked as a cop. 'You've got a game face for training all day. Unfortunately, there's not a switch that you can turn on and off. So if somebody gets in your face, you're going to attack them the way you attack your training. You don't have that much control over it. You get irritated and agitated very easily.'

When one fan asked about the secret of his success – 'What were your weak bodyparts and what did you do to bring them up?' – Wheeler replied, as if in a trance: 'My legs, my calves and my chest. I concentrate on the bodypart as I mentally masturbate, imagining my competitors watching me. This inspires me even more, as the masturbation having taken effect makes me work the muscle even more.'

If success was hard-earned, the $100,000 winners' cheques were easily squandered on fast cars, chunky jewellery, huge houses and loose women ('I was a horrible womaniser. When opportunity knocked, I opened the door'). On an express train to oblivion, he hit the buffers in 1994 when, after partying on a yacht with rappers

Dr Dre, Snoop Dogg and Queen Latifah, he crashed his $105,000 convertible Merc doing 140mph and almost died. His injuries were so bad that he needed to have his ear stitched back on, he had broken two vertebrae and had the skin on 20 per cent of his body ripped off. Almost paralysed, he was told that he may never walk again.

It is a true measure of Wheeler's nuttiness that even that near-death scare failed to stop him. Within three years he was back bodybuilding, competing at the very highest level. Only the loss of that kidney and nine life-saving operations in eleven weeks finally persuaded him to retire.

KEITH MURDOCH

The Incredible Sulk

Despite the pull of Reading legend Robin Friday, an unforgettable don't-give-a-fuck icon from my youth, Zapata-moustached Kiwi Keith Murdoch gets the final spot in this lexicon of ne'er-do-wells, psychos and eccentrics. The legendary All Black prop's claim to lunacy is his life-wreckingly disproportionate reaction to being sent home in disgrace from the 1972–73 rugby tour to Britain. Rather than simply come home and face the music after a fracas with a Cardiff security guard, he went walkabout in the Australian bush, starting an extended sulk that is still going strong more than thirty years later.

Murdoch had always been a troubled man, one of those rugby tourists who didn't have to be on tour to leave a string of broken bar-rooms in his wake. A wild man with a drink inside him, Murdoch was also hugely strong (he would trim the top of his hedge by holding out his lawnmower with a fully extended arm, and he famously towed a car up a steep hill in Dunedin by driving with one hand and gripping the tow rope out the window in the other). A perpetual thirst and eveil temper were not a happy combination and tales of Murdoch's hell-raising were legion in New Zealand even before the 1972 tour. He had, for instance, disappeared for the whole 1968 season and missed an All Black trial after a drunken adventure on a fishing boat. On tour with the All Blacks in South Africa, he had to be locked in the team bus when a Springbok made racist comments about a Maori team-mate.

In Cardiff, however, he excelled himself. The background to the day the Otago prop was ordered onto a plane from London to New Zealand is one of rugby's best-known stories. Murdoch had scored the winning try against Wales in a bad-tempered match of huge controversy thanks largely to accusations that lock Andy Haden had dived out of a lineout to win what turned out to be the winning penalty, and that J.P.R. Williams had been denied a perfectly decent try in Wales' 19–16 loss.

Earlier in the tour he had already been involved in a post-match bar-room brawl in Shrewsbury, which started when he walloped an English player on the basis that he was 'a Welsh bastard' and the night before in Cardiff he had chucked one overly voluble Welsh fan into a telephone box before wedging the door shut.

The night of the match, he had already upended a bed in the Angel Hotel in Cardiff before going in search of food after the bar had shut down. Found rummaging around in the fridges by exasperated security guard Peter Grant, a confrontation ensued in which Murdoch decked both the hapless Grant and All Blacks tour manager Ernie Todd. According to Todd, Murdoch then went upstairs and 'laid [fellow Kiwi hardman] Alex Wyllie out cold then pulled a washbasin from the wall.'

With Murdoch's rap sheet, he was always going to struggle and when Grant's battered mugshot appeared on the front pages the next day, he was on a plane home within 24 hours, dispatched in disgrace (at whose behest is hard to know – the Kiwis have always insisted it was a decision forced on them by po-faced British officials).

But rather than go home, Murdoch, who had to be sedated to get him on the plane, did a bunk in Singapore. Assuming the name 'Mr Oliver', he eluded reporters by heading for the remote North Queensland town of Port

Hedland, where he got a job working on the tuna fleet. Despite an exhaustive search, the only person who managed to track him down was legendary Kiwi journalist Terry McLean, who was given short shrift when he found him eighteen months later. McLean was sensible to demur: not only was Murdoch waving an axe but he had hack-bashing form. He once grabbed a reporter by the shirtfront in one hand and held him up under a shower; another time he and a fellow All Black prop dragged a photographer out of a bar and beat him black and blue; he even chased mild-mannered gentleman journo Ron Palenski up and down several flights of stairs in a Christchurch hotel.

Going to ground, he disappeared from view and lived as an itinerant worker in the Aussie outback until 2000, when he burst back into the media spotlight. The body of Aboriginal burglar Christopher Limerick was found down an abandoned mineshaft near the remote copper-mining town of Tennant Creek shortly after he'd tried to rob Murdoch's nearby house. True to form, Murdoch did a bunk, sparking a nationwide manhunt. No one was ever charged with Limerick's death.

A folk hero back in New Zealand where *Finding Murdoch*, a play by celebrated Auckland writer Margot McRae, recently played to packed houses, Murdoch is unwilling to be reconciled with his nation or team-mates. In 2003, several All Blacks made a video to say sorry to

Murdoch, but he only watched five minutes of it. When Ian Kirkpatrick, skipper of the 1972 side, appeared on the screen, Murdoch went bonkers and overturned the TV and video recorder. Now eligible for his pension, he refuses to forgive or forget. All hail the Incredible Sulk.